The Inner Heart of MINISTRY

Doran C. McCarty

BROADMAN PRESS
Nashville, Tennessee

Dewey Decimal Classification: 248.4
Subject Headings: CHRISTIAN LIFE // MINISTRY
Library of Congress Catalog Card Number: 85–15152
Printed in the United States of America

Unless otherwise noted, all Scripture quotations
are taken from the King James Version of the Bible.
All Scripture quotations marked RSV are taken
from the Revised Standard Version of the Bible,
copyrighted 1946, 1952, © 1971, 1973.

Library of Congress Cataloging in Publication Data

McCarty, Doran.
  The inner heart of ministry.

  1. Lay ministry. 2. Christian life—Baptist authors.
I. Title.
BV4400.M44   1985   248'.5   85-15152
ISBN 0-8054-6942-7 (pbk.)

This book is dedicated to the group of my former doctoral students who humorously (I hope) called themselves "McCarty's Clones." They have richly blessed my life and ministry.

Preface

Every Christian is called to be a minister. This calling takes some to the pulpit, some to a Sunday School class, and some to the marketplace. I have written this book hoping it would help all of us understand our ministry wherever we do it.

I have had the advantage of being a pastor and a seminary professor for enough years to see various struggles in ministry. I have seen laypersons, pastors, missionaries, and denominational workers struggle with their ministries. I hope this book helps ministers, lay and clergy, to get beyond the techniques and programs of ministering and see the inner heart of ministry.

Paul said it well: "The grace of the Lord Jesus be with you. My love be with you all in Christ Jesus. Amen" (1 Cor. 16:23-24).

DORAN C. MCCARTY

Contents

The Inner Heart of Ministry

1
Ministry Is . . .

Mr. Bennett came up to me as soon as the stranger left my table and asked, "Who is that?" When I told him that the stranger was the new minister in town, Mr. Bennett said, "Well, he sure doesn't look or talk like a minister!"

I wonder how many times that has been said about me or other ministers—especially those whose ministry is not the preaching ministry. How do you tell if someone is a minister? We recognize ministers who wear a chaplain's badge on their lapels in the hospital or have clerical collars. But who is a minister really? Is a minister someone who has a special title (Brother, Reverend, Elder, Father, Rabbi)? Complete this sentence: "A minister is. . . ."

A working definition of a minister is someone who is called by God and who responds in servanthood. How we minister and the content of our ministries is more complex, but the validity of being a minister has two parts: God's call and our servanthood. God can use whom or what He wills to minister. The psalmist spoke of God who makes His ministers a flame of fire (104:4). Even a pagan king, Cyrus, was the Lord's anointed (Isa. 45:1). Flames of fire and pagan kings may be God's ministers, but usually our questions relate to people around us who claim to be ministers.

The Calling to Be a Minister

God's calling is a mystery. It is a mystery not only because we may not understand it, but because it stirs within us a great sense of awe and fascination. The mystery is not the secret of a few who have been given exotic commands. The call to be a Christian is a call to be a minister.

Dr. William Pinson, Jr., executive director of the Baptist General Convention of Texas, wrote:

> In a sense we Christians are all ministers. The call to salvation is a call to service (2 Tim. 1:9). The vocation we are challenged to "walk worthy of " is that of ministry in Christ's name (Eph. 4:1). Our activities and relationships should be viewed as a means to or an opportunity for ministry.[1]

All Christians are ministers. When Saul (Paul) had his Damascus road experience, he asked two questions which are normative to every Christian's experience: "Who are you, Lord?" and "What will you have me do?" (see Acts 22:8-10). The first question relates to a personal knowledge of the Lord and the second question to the willingness to minister. These are not only Paul's questions but the questions of everyone who comes to faith in Christ.

The Great Commission (Matt. 28:19-20) was not a statement to the clergy but to all Christ's followers. The unique thing about Pentecost was not the communication to people of many languages but the pour-

ing out of the Spirit "upon all flesh" (Acts 2:17). Simon
Peter saw Pentecost as the beginning of the new era of
which the prophet Joel had spoken:

"And it shall come to pass afterward, that I will pour
out my spirit upon all flesh; and your sons and your
daughters shall prophesy, your old men shall dream
dreams, your young men shall see visions; And also
upon the servants and upon the handmaids in those
days will I pour out my Spirit" (Joel 2:28-29).

The spirit of God no longer fell only on priests and
the advantaged classes but on all people. All received
the power and, therefore, the obligation to minister.

The word for *church* in the New Testament is a clue
to every Christian's call to minister. The Greek word
ecclesia means "called out." The Christian church is
made up of people who have been called. The call to
salvation is a call to minister.

A Special Calling

Yes, there are special callings. Each congregation
described in the New Testament was different, and apparently there was variety in forms of ministry.[2] Whatever the form or title, it is clear that there were certain
ministers with a special calling. Pinson wrote, "The
Scriptures also reveal that some Christians receive a
special calling to certain ministry tasks. Paul felt a
very clear call to preach among the Gentiles the un-
searchable riches of Christ (Eph. 3:8). He responded to
what we would term a 'call to missions.' "[3]

The Ways God Calls

Mystery can be put in no box; it occurs in a variety
of ways. So does God's call. Moses saw a burning bush.

Samuel heard a voice in the middle of the night (1 Sam.
3). He was the instrument of David's call (1 Sam. 16).
Matthias was called to be an apostle by casting lots
(Acts 1:26). There are varieties of ways God calls people
to special ministries.

I have read the autobiographies and heard the spiritual pilgrimages told by several hundred ministers and
I have heard diverse ways God still calls. Sometimes
the call has been rather sudden and with others a long
and developing awareness. Some have experienced the
call during church services, others while walking alone
or driving in a car. There are ministers who saw the
needs of the world and knew God wanted them to minister to those needs in a special way. God gave special
gifts to people and they realize God wanted them to use
those gifts in a special way. Pastors, parents, and
friends have been instruments to make others aware of
their call by God. God has mysterious ways his wonders
to perform.

God Calls All Kinds

The mystery of God's call also relates to the kinds of
people He calls. The New Testament shows us this
mystery. There were unlettered fishermen and the
well-schooled Paul. There were commoners but Luke
appeared to be more a patrician.

God calls those with rare gifts. Albert Schweitzer
was a renowned theologian and a concert organist
before studying medicine in order to minister in Africa.
Adolph Harnack, a German theologian, could memorize a page of Greek as quickly as he turned the pages.
Francis of Assise gave up great wealth to become a
mendicant missionary.

God, in His mysterious ways, calls people of humble circumstances. Paul wrote to the Corinthians: "For consider your call, brethren; not many of you were wise according to worldly standards, not many were powerful, not many were of noble birth; but God chose . . ." (1 Cor. 1:26, RSV).

Look at the lives of the Old Testament judges and the mystery of God's call is evident. Many of them are surprise choices. Jephthah was the son of a harlot. Samson was hardly an ideal citizen. And who expected a woman prophetess, Deborah, to be called by God?

God has called mysteriously in the modern world. The great evangelist, Christmas Evans, got his name because he was left in the doorstep of an orphanage on Christmas day. Kagawa, a giant Christian of Japan, was the son of a prostitute. I was surprised when I read about my heritage of Baptists in Missouri. In the 19th century few Baptist preachers had any training. Most were farmers who started churches in nearby communities. A few couldn't even read but had to memorize Scripture passages their wives read to them. Today the churches they started are vital congregations.

Fulfilling God's Call

The validation of a minister is God's call and the response of servanthood. As important as other things are to effective ministry, these are the essentials.

Fulfilling the call to ministry means to prepare to become the most effective minister our gifts will allow. I remember when I started to college, the president of the college, Dr. John W. Dowdy, Sr., said repeatedly:

"The call to preach is a call to prepare." God gave the human species a wonderful mind, and anti-intellectualism is a blasphemy against the Creator.

Every minister has not had an open door to extended education. I am not a talented artist, but that is no reason for me to depreciate art. I am not a gifted musician, but I can sing the hymns of faith without deploring music. Despite educational limitations I can prepare myself to make full use of my gifts. J. O. Brown was born in the backwoods of Missouri in the nineteenth century. He had no chance at higher education. He read all of Spurgeon's sermons. He taught himself Hebrew and Greek. He served a congregation with all his gifts for forty years and fulfilled God's call. A call to ministry is a call to prepare and a call to servanthood.

Education is not entitlement. No one owes you a position because you have graduated from a seminary. A degree is no union card. Ministry is being called and responding to servanthood. Education occurs when we take our calling seriously enough to prepare to be the most effective minister we can be. It is then we faithfully can fulfill God's call.

There are many facets to fulfilling the call of God. The next chapter explores ways we faithfully fulfill our calling.

Notes

1. William M. Pinson, Jr., *Ready to Minister* (Nashville: Broadman Press, 1984), p. 131.

2. Compare the way the ministry was organized in Jerusalem with the arrangement in the Pastoral Epistles.

3. Pinson, p. 15.

2
Ministry Is . . . Serving

───────────── ♥ ─────────────

Albert Schweitzer, on one of his trips out of Africa, was the celebrated guest of Chicago. City officials, theologians, clergy, and press met Schweitzer's train and escorted him through the crowds only to discover he had disappeared. Searching the station, they found him carrying the bags of an elderly and feeble lady who had been unable to move through the crowd. Ministry is servanthood.

Servanthood is to help, render assistance, attend, do a good turn, offer kindness, and be devoted. Servanthood is not servility where one cringes, cowers, and fawns. It is the result of humility and concern. Servanthood means ministering.

Jesus, the Servant

Ministry as servanthood was a powerful emphasis in Jesus' life. He said, "Even as the Son of man came not to be served but to serve, and to give his life as a ransom for many" (Matt. 20:28, RSV).[1]

Paul admonished the Philippians to imitate the Lord: "Have this mind among yourselves, which is yours in Christ Jesus, who, though he was in the form of God, did not count equality with God a thing to be grasped, but emptied himself, taking the form of a servant . . ." (Phil. 2:5-7, RSV).

Jesus made servanthood the measure of greatness. He said, "Whoever would be great among you must be your servant, and whoever would be first among you must be your slave" (Matt. 20:26-27, RSV). In Jesus' parable of the talents, the master says, "Well done, good and faithful servant; you have been faithful over a little, I will set you over much; enter into the joy of your master" (Matt. 25:21, RSV). No doubt the master in the parable is providing Jesus' promise of the reward of servanthood.

Jesus showed us what servanthood is like. He helped others. He took care of the needs of the sick, sinners, mourners, and disenfranchised. Jesus washed the disciples' feet as an act of servanthood (John 13:4-11). Afterward Jesus put Lordship and servanthood together. "Know ye what I have done to you? Ye call me Master and Lord: and ye say well; for so I am. If I then, your Lord and Master, have washed your feet; ye also ought to wash one another's feet. For I have given you an example, that ye should do as I have done to you. Verily, verily, I say unto you, the servant is not greater than his Lord" (John 13:12-16).

Unfortunately, the lesson Jesus sought to teach has been lost in doctrinal arguments over foot washing being a ritual in the church. The lesson is one of servanthood which goes far beyond any one ritual. Servanthood is the road to Lordship. No wonder Paul ended the Philippian passage on Jesus taking the form of a servant with the eloquent words: "That at the name of Jesus every knee should bow, in heaven and on earth and under the earth, and every tongue confess that Jesus Christ is Lord, to the glory of God the Father" (Phil. 2:10-11, RSV).

The cross was the Great Deed of Jesus' servanthood. He gave "His life as a ransom for many." Here servanthood reached its greatest place and was crowned with thorns. Servanthood that brought a cross was no accident. Jesus patterned his life after the powerful image of the servant in the Old Testament. His life was a reflection of the Suffering Servant passage of Isaiah 52—53. Jesus' identification with the Suffering Servant was vivid among those in the apostolic era. Philip interpreted Isaiah 53:7-8 to the Ethiopian eunuch as being the "good news of Jesus" (Acts 8:32-35). First Peter 2:18-25 connects Jesus to the Suffering Servant of Isaiah.

Ministers As Servants

Jesus' servanthood is a model for his ministers, and they should "follow in His steps" (1 Pet. 2:21, RSV). Servants were commonplace in the Roman Empire in the New Testament era. The servant was often intelligent, educated, and skilled. Servants might have the care of the master's household and investments. This required the servant's faithful work. The glory of the servant was related to the honor of the master. This is why Paul could begin one of his letters, "Paul and Timothy, servants of Christ Jesus" (Phil. 1:1, RSV). To be a servant of one who was great was a position of honor. The glory did not come from the servant but the master.

Servanthood is the business of the minister. The two things that validate a minister are his call and his servanthood. I read an article by a celebrated manage-

ment expert in the American business community and
was startled by his proclamation that in industry, service is the purpose of a business. No one should know
this better than the ministers. Rather than ministers'
copying business techniques, ministers should provide
an example for business to imitiate.

Robert K. Greenleaf worked for AT&T for more than
forty years. Upon retirement he wrote a book, *Servant
Leadership,* with the subtitle, A Journey Into the Nature of Legitimate Power and Leadership. In the first
chapter, entitled "The Servant as Leader," he tells how
he came to write the book.

> The idea of *The Servant as Leader* came out of read-
> ing Herman Hesse's *Journey to the East.* In this
> story we see a band of men on a mythical journey,
> probably also Hesse's own journey. The central
> figure of the story is Leo, who accompanies the
> party as the *servant* who does their menial chores,
> but who also sustains them with his spirit and his
> song. He is a person of extraordinary presence. All
> goes well until Leo disappears. Then the group falls
> into disarray and the journey is abandoned. They
> cannot make it without Leo. The narrator, one of
> the party, after some years of wandering finds Leo
> and is taken into the Order that had sponsored the
> journey. There he discovers that Leo, whom he had
> known first as *servant,* was in fact the titular head
> of the Order, its guiding spirit, a great and noble
> *leader.*[2]

Greenleaf's interpretation is, "But to me, this story
clearly says that *the great leader is seen as servant first,*
and that is the key to his greatness."[3] In his book

Greenleaf applies this principle to business education, churches, and America.

Doesn't the story sound like Jesus and the disciples? Jesus was their servant; and when he was crucified, the disciples scattered in disarray. Now the Spirit (the Comforter Jesus promised) calls his disciples back to ministry (servanthood). No wonder the Spirit was so intimately connected to Pentecost!

The Problem

Dante, in his *Inferno,* surveyed hell and found "angels, who were not rebels, nor were faithful to God but were for themselves." That is precisely the problem: self-seeking rather than servanthood. The problem (self-seeking) is the antithesis of Jesus' operating principle, "The Son of man came not to be served but to serve" (Matt. 20:28, RSV). My college Bible professor, Dr. Joe Clapp, defined sin as "inordinate self-centeredness." That kind of sin is the *problem.* The issue is clear thus far: self-seeking versus self-giving (servanthood).

This is a minister's problem. A deacon explained about the minister their church had recently forced to resign: He "acted like he owned the church." The deacon saw the pastor as self-seeking, not self-giving.

The Association for Theological Schools, with a large grant from the Lilly foundation, did a three-year study related to the readiness of seminary students to minister. They surveyed more than five thousand laypersons, ministers, professors, and students. The criterion which was ranked number 1 was "service without regard for acclaim."[4] Jesus' principle of service is still respected in the church!

Ministers get into trouble when they act as if the

church belongs to them—its property, its program, its theology, and its money. Ministers are called to serve churches, not be served. Their glory is in their serving, not in the way they are served. Ministers should not think that others "owe them"; indeed, ministers owe service to fulfill their calling.

Self-service is not only the minister's problem; it is also the problem of institutions. An institution which promotes its existence above service is self-seeking. Institutions are founded to serve needs, not to survive. An institution which lowers its quality of service for larger budgets, endowments, or enrollees is self-seeking. Robert Greenleaf said:

> If a better society is to be built, one that is more just and more loving, one that provides greater creative opportunity for its people, then the most open course is to *raise both the capacity to serve and the very performance as servant* of existing major institutions by new regenerative forces operating within them.[5]

Inordinate self-centeredness is the plague of all people, not just ministers and institutions. Since we are all called by God to be Christians, we are all called to be ministers—that is, to serve. Servanthood means that a church does not have *a* minister (servant) but is filled with ministers (servants). They serve one another and the world. The ministers also serve the minister—not because they owe it to the minister, but they are fulfilling their own call and following Jesus' principle.

There is a subjective way we fool ourselves about service by turning serving deeds into self-service. I remember listening to a Sunday School teacher glowingly report the good feeling he had in distributing Thanksgiving baskets to the poor. He said that he hoped he would always get to do that because it always made him feel so good. Self-giving had slipped over into self-serving, and he hadn't noticed.

Self-serving is the major problem of the church's relation to the world. The church is accused of being self-seeking: always wanting money, power, prestige, and members. Whatever problems the world has, the church cannot hide its problems. A church cannot convince the world of Jesus' principle while being protective of its building and putting its own affluence—or survival—ahead of servanthood.

The Solutions

Problems have solutions. The problem of self-seeking has its solution in recapturing servanthood.

Servanthood of the Golden Rule

Everyone in Christendom knows one verse in the Sermon on the Mount—the Golden Rule: Do unto others as you would have them do unto you.[6] That is Jesus' principle of servanthood in action.

How do we serve Christ? By serving others. If we were in another person's circumstance, we know what we would want him to do for us, so servanthood is doing that for him. Jesus left no doubt what he meant in his parable when he said, "Inasmuch as ye have done it unto one of the least of these my brethren, ye have done it unto me" (Matt. 25:40).

All of us know what it means to be served. We have experienced it from our parents, our spouse, and our friends. I developed pneumonia while in college and could hardly move from my bed. Stan Bush was my roommate and a faithful servant in bringing my meals and caring for me. This was the servanthood of the Golden Rule. Stan was raised in an orphanage; he knew what it was like to be alone and to need the servanthood of others.

Servanthood as Helping

The ministry has been called one of the "helping professions." Such a title shows insight into the nature of the servanthood of the ministry. It is a compliment to the minister who is a helper. Gary Collins cites a government-sponsored study that found "that when people had personal problems only 28 percent of them went to professional counselors or clinics. Approximately 29 percent consulted their family physician and 42 percent sought help from clergymen."[7] The ministry is a "helping profession."

Being a servant isn't easy, and helping isn't easy. Collins says that "to be a disciple of Jesus Christ means that we must be willing to give up our closest relationships (Luke 14:25-26), our personal ambitions (Luke 9:23), and our possessions (Luke 14:33)."[8] Servanthood may cost.

However, helping is not just what we give. Alan Keith-Lucas wrote: "Help has in fact a second meaning, which has not to do with *what* is given, but with *how* it is given and used."[9] Some of the "hows" of giving may be technical, and we need to give them attention as servants. Jesus was the servant-helper who knew the "how" of helping. The "how" of Jesus' helping was to become God incarnate. Announcing salvation was not enough; Jesus came to live righteousness among us.

Although there are many techniques for helping, compassion and caring are essential for the servant-helper. Jesus cared. He was asleep on the boat when the disciples, fearful of the storm, awakened him and asked, "Carest thou not that we perish?" (Mark 4:38). He stilled the storm and asked why they yet had not faith. I believe He questioned their faith in Him as a caring person.

In the book *Compassion,* the authors cite Philippians 2:6-8 and comment: "Here we see the compassionate God who revealed Himself to us in Jesus Christ is the God who became a servant. Our God is a servant God."[10]

Henri Nouwen wrote:

> Real care is not ambiguous. Real care excludes in-difference and is the opposite of apathy. The word "care" finds its roots in the Gothic "Kara" which means to lament. The basic meaning of care is to grieve, to experience sorrow, to cry out with.[11]

Later he says, "Therefore, to care means first of all to be present to each other."[12] Jesus' servanthood was his being present to us and receiving our presence (Phil. 2:5-11).

Today I talked with a young man who had been terminated from his ministry position. He acknowledged his responsibility for what happened and saw the justice of it. What he was struggling with was his feeling of the lack of caring and compassion from others.

Ministers who are servants care. The minister may

not be a gifted preacher, a good administrator, or an effective evangelist; but there is no room for a minister who doesn't care. A minister can "get by" in performance of some ministry tasks, but not to care is fatal. The minister may not have all the spiritual gifts listed in Romans or 1 Corinthians, but there is no reason for the minister not to care.

Servanthood as Hospitality

Jesus called, "Come unto me, all ye that labour and are heavy laden, and I will give you rest" (Matt. 11:28). This was Jesus' hospitality and his servanthood. Heaven is where hospitality beckons. The Jerusalem church was not only a worshiping people but exhibited hospitality. The first threat to the church was over the issue of the hospitality offered to the Greeks. The church responded by appointing the Seven to care for them (Acts 6:1-6).

Servanthood is hospitality. Servants invite others to share what they have. Hospitality is being open to others and for others. Prayer is not so much storming the gates of heaven as offering hospitality to God in our hearts.

Prejudice is inhospitable. Racism is inhospitable. Elitism is inhospitable. Arrogance is inhospitable. Egotism is inhospitable. Selfishness is inhospitable. Servanthood is hospitality.

Hospitality is sharing presence with another. Hospitality is opening one's life to a mate in marriage. Hospitality is risking one's feelings with someone else. Hospitality is a cup of cold water. Hospitality is servanthood.

Ministry is . . . servanthood.

Notes

1. Note the equation of servant and minister by comparing the Revised Standard Version translation using *servant* and the King James Version using *minister.*

2. Robert K. Greenleaf, *Servant Leadership* (New York: Paulist Press, 1977), p. 7.

3. Ibid.

4. David Schuller, Milo Brekke, Merton Strommen, *Readiness for Ministry,* vol. 1 (Vandalia: The Association for Theological Schools in the United States and Canada), p. 15.

5. Greenleaf, p. 49.

6. See Matthew 7:12 and Luke 6:31.

7. Gary Collins, *How to Be A People Helper* (Ventura, California: Vision House, 1976), p. 13.

8. Ibid., p. 21.

9. Alan Keith-Lucas, *Giving and Taking Help* (Chapel Hill: The University of North Carolina Press, 1972), p. 4.

10. Donald McNeill, Douglas Morrison, Henri Nouwen, *Compassion* (Garden City: Image Books, 1983), p. 24.

11. Henri Nouwen, *Out of Solitude* (Notre Dame: Ave Maria Press, 1974), p. 33.

12. Ibid., p. 36.

3
Ministry Is . . . Showing Spirituality

Doc Adams on the television western *Gunsmoke* treated an itinerate preacher. Doc Adams was angered because the preacher insisted that Doc couldn't cure him. When Doc asked why he couldn't cure him, he got this response: "There's no hope for a preacher who has lost his faith." Of course the preacher was right; ministry is spirituality. Ministers without spirituality have nothing special to give to the church or the world.

Spiritual Beings

God made humankind spiritual beings who stand apart from the rest of the creation. That special quality, which makes us human, has been called spirit, soul, heart, and inner being. The creation story in Genesis 2 reflects God's special creative act: "And the Lord God formed man of the dust of the ground, and breathed into his nostrils the breath of life; and man became a living soul" (Gen. 2:7).

The passage that every faithful Hebrew memorized (the Shema) emphasized this inner quality. "Hear, O Israel: The Lord our God is one Lord: And thou shalt love the Lord thy God with all thine heart, and with all thy soul, and with all thy might" (Deut. 6:4-5).

Jesus repeated this to His disciples (Matt. 22:37), substituting mind for might. The three words (*heart, soul,* and *might* or *mind*) probably did not refer to distinctions but were examples of the character of Hebrew poetry to use repetition for the same truth. The point of the great passage was to call upon the spiritual character of a person's inner being.

There is a spiritual dimension to humanity. That is what it means to be created in the image of God (Gen. 1:26). God is spirit, and God created man with an inner being of spirit. Like humans, animals work and play but don't pray, worship, and build shrines. The human race has the capacity of the sacred because of the inner quality of spirit, soul, and heart.

The spiritual dimension within us means that we have a religious urge within us. As Augustine said, "Our hearts are restless till they find rest in Thee." There is a sense of the Holy within us regardless of how unholy we may act. The spiritual dimension is real. We are not prisoners of our five senses but have an inner quality which responds to what is beyond our senses. The experience of Helen Keller reveals this truth. When the letters G-O-D were first spelled in her hand she said, "I always knew about this person. I never knew what He was called before." Rather than being caught in the web of our five senses, we are able to transcend them and know something of what is beyond them. That is the gift of our spirituality.

Mediating Sources of Spirituality

While we are spiritual creatures, there are mediating sources of spirituality. These mediating sources help us to become more fully spiritual. The fulfillment of our inner being depends upon our extending awareness of this special quality. If we live like animals, our spirituality is distorted. If we live only by the five senses, we may extend our sensory perception but bankrupt our real humanity—our spirituality. Do some see trees but no forest, and see burning bushes but hear not the voice of God? Do some experience sex but not love? Do some see pictures but not beauty? Brutishness triumphs in some, spirituality in others.

Dialogue is a mediating source of spirituality. Meditation may be a form of dialogue with self. I recall walking through the woods down by a stream in my boyhood. It was a time to wonder and reflect. No doubt God was there, but I experienced dialogue with my innermost self.

There is also dialogue with others. Nothing sharpens us more than to whet your soul against another in dialogue. Another person keeps us honest against self-deceit and provides challenges to areas we have not touched. Dialogue with another self is the basis of spiritual direction.

Worship is a mediated source of spirituality. The sense of awe we experience when worship happens enriches the soul. Of course, every event called worship doesn't produce a worship experience. Do we not often go through the ritual of worship? Still we have worship to mediate the depth of spirituality so we keep our rituals with the hope that worship will happen again.

Another mediating source of spirituality is service. When we serve sacrificially, something good happens to us inwardly. When we serve and there can be no outward reward, we find inward reward. Jesus is our example; He gave Himself. Resurrection followed the cross; the crown followed service. Hearts shrivel when hands are withheld. Has a faithful Christian returned from his or her spiritual crusade of service and not known greater spiritual riches?

Study is a mediating source of spirituality. "Study to shew thyself approved unto God, a workman that needeth not to be ashamed, rightly dividing the word of truth" (2 Tim. 2:15). Holy Scripture is the mediating source from which God's people have found spiritual strength. Having the Bible on the coffee table is not enough. A simple reading is not enough. Quoting a verse is not enough. Hurling a promise at a problem is not enough. The *study* of Scripture is necessary for it to be a mediating source. My pastor steps to the pulpit and lifts the Bible above his head and says, "May these words become the Word of God for us today." It is the Spirit of God who transforms our study of the word of God into the Word of God which deepens our spirituality.

Other studies also become mediating sources of spirituality. We may study the classic devotional writings of past spiritual giants. We may study the lives of victorious Christians. Such may be mediating sources of our spirituality.

Crises are mediating sources of spirituality. Shallow living makes shallow lives. When threatened by crises, we are forced to call upon the spiritual resources within us. Prayer becomes real when we need God's strength. Faith get tough when the times get tough. Peace becomes a virtue when there are storms. Grace is visible when life is out of our control.

The Character of Spirituality

Christians don't usually doubt the reality of spirituality, but they doubt the shape of spirituality. Excessive claims and ludicrous actions in the name of spirituality has led to retreat from discussing spirituality.

Religious experiences have been described as peak and plateau experiences. Peak experiences are special and unusual spiritual experiences. People call these "mountaintop" and "life-changing" experiences. "Born again" has become a well-known phrase in American society and refers to a peak spiritual experience. Plateau spiritual experiences are characterized by repeated, long-term, and less dramatic experiences.

I grew up in a religious context which emphasized peak religious experience. Christians used theological phrases such as "born again," "saved," and the "new birth." My earliest memory of a theological debate was around the issue of the mourner's bench. The practice of the mourner's bench was an intense peak experience. The expectation was that a repentant person would spend hours (sometimes in a succession of church services) "praying through" until he had an ecstatic spiritual experience. The biblical pattern for peak spiritual experiences is Paul's Damascus road conversion experience. The experience of Paul was dramatic. Anyone who has been in the ministry very long has seen persons who have had dramatic, life-changing experiences. As important as peak spiritual experiences are, it is an unnecessary limitation to make peak experiences normative.

Plateau religious experiences are commonplace and

without the dramatic character of peak experiences. While peak experiences are more likely to happen with people who are impulsive or facing a crisis or under the burden of great guilt, plateau spiritual experiences happen more often where children are raised in religious homes and make a commitment of faith by early adulthood. It seems as though the energy manifest suddenly in a peak experience is spread out over many less dramatic experiences.

Spirituality has been described as privatized or social. Privatized spiritual experiences refer to highly religious and "churchy" experiences which emphasize individual values. Among these values are personal honesty, truthfulness, and piety. These values are important to build inner character for people. These are building blocks for a spiritual life and righteousness.

Advocates of social spirituality have ridiculed privatized spirituality since this emphasis often ignores social issues in the community and society. Social spirituality sees God as the Lord of all the world and not just the church.

I am always saddened when I see advocates of social spirituality insensitive to values of private spirituality. However, while private spirituality furnishes the building blocks of character, sin is demonic and transcends the individual. Reinhold Niebuhr's title of his Gifford lectures can be descriptive: Moral Man in Immoral Society. Spirituality is myopic when it does not reach beyond its own personal piety to bring the spiritual value of justice to the world. I have been impressed that nearly all the prayers I've heard from Roman Catholics have included prayer for the poor. Of course, prayer isn't the end of concerned action, but it may help us be sensitive to the needs of those beyond ourselves. After all, a privatized spirituality which is concerned only with "me, my wife, my sons James and John, us four and no more" is shallow spirituality.

Is the character of spirituality conceptual or affective? Some see spiritual as basically having the right ideas (conceptual), and for others spirituality is deep feelings (affective). Spirituality based on distorted ideas is dangerous, as the massacre of Jonestown showed us. Spirituality also relates to feelings of the will. A person who has right words but distorted feelings is also dangerous. This is the condition which brings religious persecution and political oppression. This is why we have the admonition to "test the spirits to see whether they are of God" (1 John 4:1, RSV). Ideas without the spiritual power of courage are only shadows reflecting from divine fires but bring no heat from their isolation to a spiritually frozen world.

Spirituality is not either/or. Peak spiritual experiences need to be followed by plateau spirituality. Privatized spirituality needs to be the foundation for the sensitivity of social spirituality. Mindless feelings should become informed spirituality.

Spiritual Language and Spirituality

We are all familiar with religious language. After all, every discipline has its own language. Schools now offer courses in computer language. Maybe we should offer a course in religious language to clear up confusion and enrich spirituality. Imagine how many have heard preachers talk about grace or redemption but have never heard such spiritual language explained.

Spiritual language is made up of special words or

common words used in a special way. Ian Ramsey says that religious language is "odd language"—language used in a different way. When an automobile advertisement says, "Datsun saves," it hardly means the same things as an evangelical preacher who says, "Jesus saves."

Spiritual language is metaphorical. It appeals more to the imagining than computerlike data. All great literature is highly metaphorical. That is because the power of the image of a metaphor transcends the power of literatism. T. S. Eliot said, "Genuine poetry can communicate before it is understood." Psalm 23 has that transcendent power as it portrays "The Lord is my shepherd." Spiritual language is not just words of the English (or some other language) language which communicates ideas but is uncommon (odd) language that communicates the depths of the soul.

Paul knew what this meant when he wrote: "Likewise the Spirit helps us in our weakness; for we do not know how to pray as we ought, but the Spirit Himself intercedes for us with sighs too deep for words. And he who searches the hearts of men knows what is the mind of the Spirit, because the Spirit intercedes for the saints according to the will of God" (Rom. 8:26-27, RSV).

Spiritual language is also a serious problem. It is by necessity vague. It can be easily misinterpreted. Metaphors can image great truths or mean nothing. Spiritual language is subject to misuse. When we cannot explain something, we may resort to spiritual language rather than seeking further for the answer. We may drape the word-shroud of "mystery" over what we are not willing to examine. Spiritual language can even be a coverup. How often we have heard people invoke "the Lord's will" to cover up their mistakes or to get people to follow them without question.

Exercise care! A person who speaks with spiritual language is not necessarily spiritual. It nears the demonic when a person speaks the language of Zion but is only "full of sound and fury, signifying nothing."

The Pilgrim's Progress

John Bunyan's famous *The Pilgrim's Progress* is one of those beautiful pieces of literature in metaphors. He portrays a Christian traveling on the way to City Beautiful and the problems the pilgrim has along the way. There is the worldly city, the slough of despair and wrong companions making the way challenging and difficult.

We are pilgrims on a worldly journey between the cradle and grave, but we are also spiritual pilgrims. On the pilgrimage we struggle with principalities and powers (Rom. 8:38). The path of spirituality may be the less traveled road that makes all the difference. Spirituality is no wayside inn on an obscure road or a rest stop on an interstate highway; it is a pilgrimage. We go from place to place but with a purpose. Wherever we become comfortable in the wayside inn, we have ceased to be the pilgrim on the way. However far we have come is a cause for celebration but no reason for stopping; the pilgrimage goes on. People who act as if they have arrived have forgotten they are pilgrims. "Go and grow" is the motto of the pilgrim.

Spiritual Growth

We are not born fully spiritual, neither in our natural birth nor our second birth. Indeed, Paul told the Corinthians: "But I, brethren, could not address you as spiritual men, but as men of the flesh, as babes in Christ. I fed you with milk, not solid food; for you were not ready for it; and even yet you are not ready" (1 Cor. 3:1-2, RSV). We are on the pilgrimage from domination by the "flesh" to the Lordship of the Spirit. Spiritual growth is the work of the Christian life.

How do we grow spiritually? We have some obvious answers: worship, prayer, study of Scripture, Christian service. The temptation is to say that if I want to grow spiritually at a faster rate, I can do more of these things; I can go to church twice as often, memorize more verses, etc. We may believe that a person who does more of these things is more spiritually mature. Spiritual growth and maturity do not come from intense repetition. A thirty-year-old is not more mature than an eight-year-old because he plays hide-and-seek more often than the eight-year-old. The thirty-year-old is more mature because of the qualitative difference in his activity. The thirty-year-old takes on responsibility which the eight-year-old cannot and should not do.

Spiritual growth for the eight-year-old may come by memorizing Scripture; but for the thirty-year-old, spiritual growth more likely comes by service to others: teaching, witnessing, or helping the needy. Spiritual growth is related to physical and psychological growth. Sexuality relates to the spirituality of the thirty-year-old but not the eight-year-old. Psychologically the eight-year-old may be beginning to identify with some group (us Baptists can whip you Methodists). The spiritual growth of the thirty-year-old may have moved beyond sole identification with a group to recognize his responsibility to those beyond his group.

This means that spiritual growth is related to life's stages. Spirituality to the eight-year-old may simply be not stealing his schoolmate's marbles. The spirituality of the thirty-year-old may relate to his responsibility to his wife and profession as he deals with an early adult life crisis or passage.

There are disciplines which help us on our pilgrimage of spiritual growth. Richard Foster has identified these disciplines for spiritual growth as inward disciplines, outward disciplines, and corporate disciplines.[1]

The inward disciplines are meditation, prayer, fasting, and study. Thomas Merton wrote: "To meditate is to exercise the mind in serious reflection."[2] Activistic American society makes meditation difficult. Even when we are alone, we are likely to be wired up to a radio or tape player. Time is needed for tranquility within in order to meditate. Prayer is our communion with God. It is active conversation with God. Fasting has been a stranger in Protestant traditions. For centuries it was a way to center one's thoughts on God and a means of self-discipline. Study of the Scripture, the nature of reality, the lives of others, and the way others perceive their situation brings depth to our lives and material to be used in meditation.

The outward disciplines, according to Foster, are simplicity, solitude, submission, and service. Simplicity refers to a life-style marked by practicality rather the prestige of consumerism. Solitude speaks of the

aloneness (not loneliness) we need. Henri Nouwen
wrote:

> A life without a lonely place, that is, a life without
> a quiet center, easily becomes destructive. When we
> cling to the results of our actions as our only way of
> self-identification, then we become possessive and
> defensive and tend to look at our fellow human be-
> ings more as enemies to be kept at a distance than
> as friends with whom we share the gifts of life.[3]

Submission is being obedient to God. We may also
need to submit ourselves to one another. Service is our
giving to others. Spirituality grows when we reach
beyond ourselves.

The corporate disciplines are confession, worship,
guidance, and celebration. Confession need not be in a
booth or embarrassing the public with lurid details.
Confession is purging the soul. Worship may occur pri-
vately, but it is no private affair. Worship may be in-
tensely personal, but it is a corporate act. Guidance
refers to letting others help us on our spiritual journey.
Spirituality has an element of celebration because it
brings joy. Celebration is an act of thankfulness and
honoring God's gifts to us.

The undisciplined life is a brutish sort of life and not
the best for which God made us. The disciplined life
exercises our spiritual nature of self-control.

Spiritual Direction

Spiritual direction takes place when we ask someone
to be our guide in reflection on our spiritual pilgrimage. Spiritual direction on a regular basis is not com-

monplace. Given the importance of spirituality, we need someone to open up new vistas to us and keep us from self-deception. The hunger of the soul calls for another to feed us. I have found that both being and having a spiritual director is spiritually enriching.

There are several kinds of spiritual direction. Corporate spiritual direction is what we experience in worship. Scriptures, hymns, and sermons provide us with spiritual direction. Sometimes worship strikes deep within us, touching points of our spiritual growth. At other times we wish we could call out for worship leaders to stop and deal with our issues.

Occasional direction occurs when we take advantage of an encounter with someone to "talk through" where we are on our spiritual pilgrimage.[4] Some have made spiritual "retreats," meeting with someone for a few days for spiritual reflection.

Personal direction takes place when we choose someone to be our spiritual director. The task of the spiritual director is not to lecture on spirituality but to ask questions to find out where we are and to probe us in order to stimulate our reflection about our spiritual pilgrimage.[5]

Paul must have seen himself as a kind of spiritual director. He wrote in Romans 1:11, "For I long to see you, that I may impart to you some spiritual gift to strengthen you." The principle of spiritual direction was inherent in his letter to the Corinthians when he told them he had to feed them on milk rather than meat (1 Cor. 3:1-2).

The spiritual director is a person who shares personhood and interfaces with another. What I have called "soul rubbing" occurs when two people share their spiritual selves with each other. It is a serious relationship, to be entered with commitment.

The Church Wants Spiritual Leaders

The ministry of Paul and Barnabas was once described as "strengthening the souls of the disciples" (Acts 14:22, RSV). Churches want spiritual ministers who can strengthen the souls of the members. Some unfortunate churches have taken the spirituality of a prospective minister for granted and have looked at his speaking fluency or administrative skills. The unique contribution of ministers is their spirituality. Wherever a minister goes, there will be persons with administrative gifts; but the minister has to be a spiritual leader.

The spiritual minister transcends the mob and sees beyond the feelings of the moment or even the era. The spiritual minister is above the pettiness of momentary squabbles. The spiritual minister feels the hurts of others: the disappointed, the injured, the ill, the bereaved, and the oppressed. Anyone can be caught by the mob's fever pitch, pettiness, and callousness; but spirituality has its own kind of radar that penetrates beyond these.

Terry Holmes distinguished between two kinds of ministers—the shaman and the logician.[6] The shaman was in touch with the inner world, the unconscious. The logician dealt with ideas and drew logical conclusions. While ideas and logic cannot be abandoned, the spiritual minister is the sensitive shaman in touch with more than outward manifestations. The spiritual minister "feels" as well as thinks. It is what some have called "the pastor's heart."

Churches want their ministers to be spiritual and for

it to show in all their ministry and lives. Spirituality
needs to come from the pulpit. The sermon needs to
reveal compassion and concern as well as logical ideas.
Church members want the minister to be spiritual
when visiting their homes. William Barclay said, "The
pastor's visit should be more than a social call."[7]
Churches want a minister's spirituality to show in the
minister's home, the restaurant, and the ball field.

Churches cry out to their ministers as Simon Peter
answered the Lord, "To whom shall we go? thou hast
the words of eternal life" (John 6:68). Where will the
church go for spirituality if not to the minister?

Ministry is . . . spirituality.

Notes

1. See Richard Foster, *Celebration of Discipline* (San Francisco:
Harper & Row Publishers, 1978).

2. Thomas Milton, *Spiritual Direction and Meditation* (College-
ville, Minn.: The Liturgical Press, 1960), p. 43.

3. Henri Nouwen, *Out of Solitude* (Notre Dame: Ave Maria Press,
1960), p. 24.

4. Jean Laplace speaks of occasional, collective, correspondence,
and permanent direction. See *Preparing for Spiritual Direction,* pp.
140-165.

5. See my booklet *A Guide for Spiritual Directors.*

6. Terry Holmes, *The Minister As Priest* (New York: The Seabury
Press, 1978).

7. William Barclay, *William Barclay: A Spiritual Autobiography*
(Grand Rapids: William B. Eerdmans Publishing Co., 1977), p. 76.

4
Ministry Is . . . Leading

———————————— ♥ ————————————

I asked one of my ministry classes to mark a list of subjects they wished to cover in the class. To my amazement, no student marked "leadership." When I asked the class about it, some remarked that they thought that selecting leadership would not seem humble.

Ministry is . . . leading. The call of God is a call to be a leader. Ministers are to lead others to faith, believers to growth, and the church to faithful service. In the Bible a call from God was a call to leadership. Abraham, Moses, Samuel, David, Peter, Paul, and Timothy were called to be leaders. Those whom God calls are leaders—in servanthood, spirituality, and humility.

Ministers are leaders by virtue of their preparation. A seminary graduate ranks in the 98th percentile in education in the world. Good education is preparation for leadership.

Leadership Through Service

Ministry is . . . leading. Leadership in the ministry comes by serving others. A minister's leadership does not come from being born to aristocracy or by ordination. We fulfill our call to leadership by our servanthood. Leading involves power. I know the reluctance of

ministers to talk about the subject of power; it sounds
dirty and worldly. However, all persons have power,
and they "loan" it to the person they perceive to be
their leader. A minister cannot fulfill the calling to
ministry without accepting these "loans" of power
from others. Good ministers treat these "loans" with
respect and honor. Young ministers often mistake
these "loans" in two ways. They see the "loans" as
their possession rather than being stewards of the
loans of power. Other ministers realize that they are
only stewards of power and feel powerless because they
only see real power as absolute. A part of ministers'
servanthood is to be faithful stewards of these loans of
power. When people perceive ministers acting arro-
gantly with their power rather than servants, they recall their "loans" of power.

Education helps a minister know how to be a leader.
However, greater education does not necessarily mean
enlarged leadership. Ministers who depend solely on
their education for their leadership forfeit greater
leadership which comes by their calling and servanthood. The business community has discovered that
education isn't all that is needed for success in business
leadership. After extensive research, J. Sterling Livingston wrote:

> Lack of correlation between scholastic standing and
> success in business may be surprising to those who
> place a premium on academic achievement. But
> grades in neither undergraduate nor graduate
> school predict how well an individual will perform
> in management.[1]

During seventeen years of teaching in seminaries, I have had many churches contact me wanting information concerning alumni they were considering for a position. None has ever asked me about prospects' grade point in school. They want to know if the person will serve their church well. Leadership comes through service, and education helps a minister know how to serve.

A minister has to pay the price of service in order to be a leader. I recall a young minister complaining to me because he had not been chosen to serve on the state convention executive board and asked how he could get recognition in the denomination. I told him what I had seen other ministers do. They had begun by accepting a youth committee job or some other inconspicuous job in the local association. After they had taken initiative and worked hard to create a good program, they began to receive recognition and were elected to more conspicuous responsibilities. First they had to pay the price of leadership. A person does not unite with a church and immediately become elected as a deacon. He has to show that he is willing to serve in the church.

When a person becomes pastor of a church, the church does not immediately give the pastor all the leadership. Parishioners want to see if the new pastor will serve the needs of the church faithfully before they turn over too much of the leadership.

Factors in Leading

The basic factor in leading is servanthood. People want to know if you will serve them and their church or institution. The minister who is perceived as self-

serving rather than as a servant will not be granted
leadership. Service manifests itself in several factors.
Some of these are information, physical strength or
attractiveness, personality, money, and position.

The person who serves others with valuable information becomes a leader. An accountant on a budget committee can become a leader if people believe that the
accountant is trying to serve the good or the organization instead of being self-seeking. Albert Einstein
didn't become a leader by running for an office but by
having an unusual wealth of knowledge and trying to
help people understand the world in which they live.

Physical strength and attractiveness are factors in
leadership. If a group sees that a person will use a
leadership position to enhance self but will do nothing
for those he or she is supposed to lead, the group will
not allow the most handsome man or beautiful woman
to lead. However, if all other factors are equal, a group
may choose on the basis of the physical. Sometimes
groups make the mistake of choosing only on the basis
of the physical and later have to admit that they made
a mistake.

One of the sad situations in life is the person who
gets by for a while on a physical advantage and doesn't
grow personally. I have seen this happen to ministers;
they get by for a while but end up disastrously. Often
they don't develop the skills which they need for more
challenging ministry situations and find that they
can't cope or can't meet more demanding expectations.
They have let people serve them but have not learned
how to serve.

Some have extraordinary personalities which are
winsome and gregarious. People are attracted to them.

Again, they may get a position because people don't investigate thoroughly enough to see what is behind the winsome personality. Unfortunately, many of these end up like those who are physically attractive. They depend upon their natural gifts rather than growing. Later people see that they are extractive rather than serving and begin to distrust them. The church may begin to think that the person is too "slick." When this person learns how to serve, he or she becomes an excellent leader. But he can only get by so long talking about servanthood; sooner or later he has to serve.

People who have money are wanted for leadership. Many of them have already proved their competence. Money is important to most people and institutions. However, I have seen the wealthy passed over for leadership positions because people were convinced that they were only using their wealth to get the position and would not use it to serve the people or institution. I recall a candidate for the Senate who advertised how many corporate boards he was on. He was badly beaten in the election although his party swept the nation. Servanthood is still the key ingredient in leading.

The leadership positions a person has had are key factors in being chosen for leadership. A person who holds a significant position (or who has held one) is sought after for leadership. An alert group will try to determine if the person is just a climber or if he has proven to be trustworthy and willing to serve. People don't want to be stepping-stones but to be served. When a person serves well and leaves, people don't feel betrayed as though they had only been a stepping-stone, but rejoice in the new opportunity their leader has received.

Sometimes persons become leaders in spite of not having a great deal to offer in any of these areas. They may become leaders because they are brokers of these factors. They make the best use of the gifts of others. This works for many as long as they are perceived as trying to serve well the good of the church or institution.

A person may gain leadership because of tenure more than because the person is gifted. Never is servanthood more evident. I have seen people with long tenure who continued to be passed over. The one ingredient that is indicated by electing someone because of tenure is that he or she has been a faithful servant across the years.

Leadership Is Risking

One of the celebrated examples of leadership risking took place after World War II. The leadership at Montgomery Ward believed that there would be another depression like that in 1929 and kept millions of dollars in reserve. Sears invested in new stores and products. As a result of Sears' being willing to risk, they became the dominant company and later Montgomery Ward was taken over by Mobil Oil Company. Good leading requires risking.

Churches have gone "out of business" because they were unwilling to risk in new buildings and ministries. Pastors have become like dinosaurs because they stayed the way they were and refused to risk new ways and new ideas.

Jesus risked. He risked opposing tradition. He risked when he associated with sinners. He risked trying to bring salvation to a world. He paid for his risks on the cross, but there would never have been a resurrection without his risk taking. Paul risked. He went into towns knowing that the result might be imprisonment or beatings. He risked when he appealed to Caesar, but that was his way of preaching the gospel in Rome.

Risk is necessary for growth. We grow intellectually when we must risk exposing our ideas and considering new ideas. If a person is to seek a position, he or she must risk defeat and rejection. Marriage is a blessed institution, but it carries great risks. The present divorce rate (even among ministers) attests to the risk. Children are enriching, but there is great risk with every child: birth defects, accidents, health, behavioral problems.

Leaders lay their leadership on the line every time they are called upon to take a risk. Part of the problem is that they risk themselves. They risk their ego, identity, and sense of OKness. People have difficulty risking because they perceive what might happen to them. The leaders who do well at risking have a strong sense of their identity and feel OK about themselves. They are strong enough to stand the strain of risking and even of losing.

The leader who does well at risking needs a support network which helps him examine options and look at ways of problem solving. The support group also offers emotional (and perhaps other kinds of) support. Without the support group the leader is isolated to his or her own thinking and has no one with whom to walk through the risk situation. The support group cannot be measured in terms of numbers; nor is it made up of just anyone who says a kind word. The support group must be made up of "significant others" of the risk taker. One of the most important parts of a minister's support group is the spouse and family. But the minister faces disaster in ministry as well as at home if there are not other persons in the support group.

The fear of loss is a factor in risking. Perhaps nothing shows us as clearly what is "holy" to us than what we are willing to risk. Good risk takers will risk everything except what is "holy" to them. We may find that peace, money, and relationships are "holy" to us as well as the Kingdom of God.

What people really want to know is whether what they hold to be sacred is in good hands with you. This question tests the minister's servanthood in risk taking. I was told of a minister who put great pressure on his congregation to give sacrificially. He illustrated his own giving by bringing his favorite hunting guns to church, placing them on the communion table, and saying that they would be sold and the money given to the church as his sacrificial offering. Later the congregation found that he had already arranged for the staff to buy the guns and present them to him as a gift. Within a few weeks the pastor was gone from the church. They felt that he was not honest in risking and serving.

How much are you willing to risk? There are people who get pleasure out of risking. The gambling business depends on this quality and greed. The person who simply likes the excitement of risk taking is no servant and will eventually find that he is out in no man's land alone.

How much are you willing to risk to be a leader? I once read that Desi Arnaz said he would give all the money he had except enough to put on one pilot show

to have a golf swing like Lee Trevino. There is a price
to pay for risking. There is no reason to consider risking unless you are willing to pay the price. Also, there
is no need to risk if your risking is not done to serve
others. People do not want you to risk what is sacred
to them for your own aggrandizement.

Intentional Ministry

Leading in ministry means being intentional in ministry actions. Intentional ministry occurs when a person consciously and purposefully intervenes into an
ongoing process to bring change.

The incarnation was God's supreme intervention
into human history. It was part of the "plan of the
ages," as W. O. Carver called it. The result of this divine intervention changed the destiny of the world.

Ministry can be reactive or proactive. Reactive ministry reacts to situations. Proactive ministry looks to
the future and tries to determine what the situations
will be. Proactive ministry sets an agenda rather than
reacting to the agenda of a given situation.

A doctoral candidate had been pastor of a church in
a rural community for nine years. When his peers
asked him why he didn't improve the ministries of the
church, the pastor related the opposition from laypeople who were very traditional. His peers encouraged
him to take the initiative to bring about needed
changes. With their encouragement he intervened in
the situations which needed to be changed. During the
next year, the church experienced more improvements
and growth than during the pastor's previous nine
years. He had become intentional and had intervened.

Four Alternatives in Ministry

There are four ways to approach ministry. The first two approaches seldom bring progress. When they are used, the ministry is not intentional and the results are seldom productive. The other two methods will be productive if they are both used.

1. Ministry by Accident

Some stumble into ministry opportunities and do things they had never intended and for which they had never planned. They have no goals, so the ministry they do is accidental, not purposeful and intentional. A pastor was walking down the sidewalk in a small town when a boy ran into him with his bicycle. The pastor angrily told the boy, "If you don't straighten up, the devil's going to get you." The boy thought about it and joined the other church in town. The pastor was only expressing his anger, but the result was an accidental ministry he hadn't intended.

2. Ministry by Intimidation

Ministers may let others rule them by threats spoken or unspoken. Or they may be intimidated by shame to do ministry which was unplanned. A deacon chastised a pastor because he had not been to visit the deacon's infirmed mother. As a result of the intimidation by the deacon, he visited the ill woman and rendered ministry to her.

3. Ministry by Intervention

Ministers need to see situations that exist and look for future possible situations and plan to intervene into them with ministries. This requires planning and gathering of resources. Another minister knew there would be great change in the community during the next decade. He led the church to develop a long-range plan to keep up with the new opportunities which the changes would make. As a result the church was ready to build when they needed to build and add staff and programs.

A pastor saw that several young people in the church would graduate from high school in the next two years. Most of them would go to college and face situations they had never experienced in their small town and for which they were unprepared. The pastor started a special class to prepare the youth for their college experiences. These are ministries by intervention.

4. Ministry by Serendipity

Serendipity means an occurrence or opportunity of complete surprise. Ministry by serendipity is different from ministry by accident. When a minister has a goal and then a special opportunity arises which gives an opportunity to fulfill that goal, the result is ministry by serendipity. The difference is the intentionality which gives the minister the opportunity to intervene and fulfill the goal when the situation arises.

A pastor had wanted his church to reach into the community with ministries but had no success convincing the congregation to do so. After a tornado in the town, the Red Cross asked the church to be in charge of distributing clothing to the storm victims. The church responded, and the people felt so good about that outreach that they began to look for other means to minister to the community. The pastor had a goal and took advantage of an opportunity to achieve the goal.

Developing Priorities

Regardless of how intentional you are, you can only intervene into a limited number of situations. You must develop priorities.

First of all, examine your theological priorities. There is a reason for this being plural; most of us have several theological priorities. Our theological priorities should dictate our interventions more than the convenience of situations or the availability of denominational programs.

Needs determine our priorities for intervention. When we see a potential need, if we are intentional, we will begin to plan to meet the need. Plans that meet low priority needs are not worthy to be carried out.

Since we have limited resources of time and money, we need to develop sequential priorities. While our goal may be to enlarge the Sunday School, we may have to provide more classes before we can do so. We will have to sequence our priorities.

A church may not be as enthusiastic about our first priority as we would like, but they will support our second priority. We also have to determine what the supported priorities are, or our intervention may be premature and become thwarted.

Intentionality means that we must look at the long term. We will need to take time to get others to share our priorities and support them.

A Process for Intentional Ministry

Leadership necessitates intentional ministry. Where there is no intentionality, leadership cannot be achieved.

Determine what your objectives are, based on your theology and the needs you see. These serve as the magnetic pole which guides you. You will need to examine these from time to time as a reminder of what you hope to achieve.

When you have your objectives identified, you can set goals based on these objectives. Good goals will be specific, attainable, and measurable.

Goals require strategies and actions. You will have to do many different tasks to reach each goal. Some strategies will be disappointing; others will only nudge things toward the goal. It will take many actions to reach any one goal. Don't give up when one action does not achieve the goal, regardless of how good that action might be.

Finally, you need to be able to evaluate what you have accomplished toward reaching your goals. Set up the criteria for success and the process you will use to determine whether you have reached the goal. Many ministers have been discouraged because they did not bother to evaluate what really happened. Others deceive themselves because, without proper evaluation, they declare that goals were met.

Ministry is . . . leading. Leaders must have an idea about where they are going or they won't be effective leaders. Intentionality is important to leading. Intentionality requires intervention into situations. Moses was a leader, but he had to intervene with God and his people. As a leader Moses had to plan intentionally, which explains why he sent spies into Canaan. Moses was a minister of God.

Ministry is . . . leading.

Note

1. J. Sterling Livingston, "Myth of the Well Educated Manager," *Path Toward Personal Progress: Leaders Are Made Not Born* (Boston: Harvard Business Review: 1983).

5
Ministry Is . . . Blessing

━━━━━━━━━━━━━━━ ♥ ━━━━━━━━━━━━━━━

Ministry is . . . blessing. There is great spiritual hunger for blessings. Note the throngs that line a papal cavalcade and crowd into St. Peter's huge square for the pope's weekly appearance. People hunger for a blessing.

Blessing is the business of the minister. First Peter 3:9 instructs us to "bless, for to this you have been called" (RSV). People call ministers to serve them because they believe God will bless them through the minister. Ministry is . . . blessing. Israel believed that God blessed the king and they received blessings from the king. Unlike their neighbors, Israel did not believe that the king automatically had the blessings of God but only when the king's actions were a blessing to the people.

Saul fell into disfavor with God and David was blessed with anointment as king (1 Sam. 16:12-13). When David sinned against his people (and God), Nathan brought the message of a curse (not a blessing) on David which was shared by his people (see 2 Sam. 12, 24). Priests were blessed by God and were to bless the people. There was even an oral blessing the priests were to pronounce over the people:

"The Lord said to Moses, 'Say to Aaron and his sons,
Thus you shall bless the people of Israel: you shall say
to them,/The Lord bless you and keep you:/The Lord
make his face to shine upon you, and be gracious to
you:/The Lord lift up his countenance upon you, and
give you peace' " (Num. 6:22-26, RSV).

Ministry is . . . blessing.

Cursing seems to come more easily for those in the
Puritan tradition. Wherever there is legalism, it is easy
to forget that "Christ redeemed us from the curse of the
law" (Gal. 3:13). Some churches have been preoccupied
with cursing at times with their anathemas and excom-
munications. Other groups have used shunning as a
form of cursing. It appears to be a temptation to curse
sinners—gamblers, prostitutes, drunkards—and forget
that ministry is blessing.

Blessing appears to be overlooked by the scholars
too. Paul Pruyser laments that after looking in the
index of one hundred books only two had references to
blessing. Claus Westermann said that only one Old
Testament theologian had seen the importance of the
idea of blessing in the Old Testament. Blessings are
important, for people tend to live them out. Blessings
give people a sense of self-worth. They bring hope to
people struggling in the mire of the human situation.

A friend of mine, after frustrating experiences in the
pastorate, went into management counseling. After he
became successful in his new vocation, I asked him
what he would do differently in the pastorate now. His
answer was that he would affirm people. He said that
people would do significant Christian service and he
took it for granted because they were Christians. But
he appreciated being told that he had preached a good

sermon and even being paid for it. He had discovered
that ministry is . . . blessing.

The Power of the Curse

Primitive religion emphasizes the power of the curse.
Through magic and incantations the shaman or witch
doctor believes he can put a curse on people. We have
all heard of the voodoo hex. The shamans and their
followers believe their powers to curse are real.

There is a story in the Ras Shamra tablets, which
archaeologists discovered, about a man and his son
meeting an enemy. The enemy began to shout curses
at the man, who threw his son to the ground so that the
curses would pass over him and leave him unaffected.
He believed in the reality of the spoken word and
curses.

The most interesting story in the Bible regarding
cursing is that of Balaam, who was hired by Balak to
curse Israel (Num. 23—24). When Balaam stood on the
mountain above the camp of Israel so that his curses
might fall on them, he opened his mouth but only blessings would come out, not curses.

Primitive religion had only one remedy for a curse:
to lay a greater curse on the one cursing you. Jesus
changed the formula. The Christian's defense against
the curse of an enemy is to "bless them that curse you"
(Matt. 5:44).

The Power of Blessing as Seen in Scripture

Blessing is a central issue in Scripture. The human
race shares the curse of Genesis 3:14. Ever since then
humanity has tried to rid itself of the curse, receive the
blessing of God, and return to the former blessed state.

God did bless certain people with special blessings. Although blessings were closely related to God's election, they were also related to responses of faith and righteous acts (justice).

God also gave some the power to bless. In the framework of the Bible, this began with Abraham. "I will bless thee, and make thy name great; and thou shalt be a blessing: And I will bless them that bless thee, and curse him that curseth thee: and in thee shall all families of the earth be blessed" (Gen. 12:2-3). According to the Abrahamic covenant he was to receive God's blessings and to be a blessing.

The New Testament gave a new dimension to blessing. Instead of cursing enemies, the Christian is to bless enemies (Matt. 5:43-44; 1 Pet. 3:9). One of the reasons given for this kind of blessing is that it is the way God acts. Matthew 5:45 continues to speak of blessing enemies by saying, "So that you may be sons of your Father who is in heaven; for he makes his sun rise on the evil and on the good, and sends rain on the just and on the unjust" (RSV).

The great example of this was Jesus Christ, whom the world did not accept (John 1:11), who was the stone the builders rejected (Mark 12:10) and who was despised, rejected, and crucified (Heb. 12:2). The Incarnation was God offering blessing to those who curse Him. "For God so loved the world that he gave his only begotten Son" (John 3:16).

Beatitude means blessing. The Beatitudes of the Sermon on the Mount was Jesus' blessings on the unlikely. The poor were unlikely prospects for blessings. In Jesus' day (and ours) the poor were rejected. The meek and merciful won no popularity contests in Jesus' day (hardly different from ours).

Another unlikely group Jesus blessed were the peacemakers. In fact, peacemakers still have trouble in the world. Throughout Jesus' ministry he blessed the unlikely: poor fishermen, prostitutes, lepers, and tax collectors. If blessing the unlikely is Jesus' work, the promise in Matthew 24:46 is important: "Blessed is that servant whom his master when he comes will find so doing." Ministry is . . . blessing.

The Power of Blessing

Lyle Schaller talks about "Silver Beavers and Dead Rats" in a section of one of his books. He relates how the Boy Scouts of America have elaborate ceremonies in which they honor persons who have given exceptional service to scouting. He compares that to the way many churches only criticize good efforts. The Boy Scout award is called the "Silver Beaver Award," and Schaller dubs the churches' misguided efforts as the "Dead Rat Award."

There is power in blessing, and the church should not miss using its power since Jesus used it so effectively. When a person leaves a worship service or the pastor leaves a home, people should feel blessed, not dirty.

Blessing is the power to heal. Broken hearts have been healed by the power of blessing. Shattered spirits have been healed by the power of blessing. Myron Madden has an interesting insight: "Ira Levin, in *Rosemary's Baby,* shows how the curse produces a monster. He also indicates at the close of his novel that love and blessing start the slow process of transformation of the monster child into a person." A demonic curse is unlikely to be driven out by a human curse but by a blessing. That is God's way. He did not bring about redemption through a curse but by a blessing—Jesus Christ.

Blessing is the power to free. Through Christ's blessing we have been liberated from the prison camp of the law of sin and death (Rom. 8:2). People may not feel free for fear of a "curse" if they don't do something right. The results of this fear of a curse are inhibitions which prevent us from service. Jesus never suffered from such a fear. Because he was confident that he was blessed by the Father, He reached out to minister to the unlovely and unlikely, even when it was unpopular.

All want to share the power of blessings in our lives. Perhaps there was no more poignant plea in the Bible than that of Esau to his father after Isaac had been tricked into giving his blessing to Jacob. "Esau said to his father, 'Have you but one blessing, my father? Bless me, even me also, O my father' " (Gen. 27:38, RSV).

Ways to Bless

The greeting and the benediction were the two most ritualized ways of offering a blessing in the Bible. The most common form of both was *shalom,* the Hebrew word for peace. This practice has been somewhat popularized in the past few years in what has been called "passing the peace." The first person turns to another and says, "Peace be with you," to which the second responds with, "And also with you." Afterward the second person repeats to another and this is continued until all have participated.

When angels appeared to the shepherds on the occasion of Jesus' birth, they dispelled their fear of a curse by blessing them with the words, "On earth peace, good will toward men" (Luke 2:14). Jesus instructed the seventy to use the "peace" greeting when they went out on their preaching mission: "Whatsoever house you enter, first say, Peace be to this house!" (Luke 10:5). Paul's statement of blessing was often "grace and peace" (1 Cor. 1:3).

The ascension story is the marvelous example of a benediction. Jesus' life had begun with the angel's blessing of peace. At his ascension, Jesus' last act was described this way by Luke: "While he blessed them, he parted from them" (Luke 24:51, RSV).

Our own worship services would be enhanced with the pronouncement of the blessing of God rather than a breezy introduction by the pastor or music director. Likewise, a congregation would benefit from a benediction at the conclusion of worship which would send them out into the world with affirmation. Too many so-called benedictions are repetitions of the sermon outline or the announcements for the week.

Invocations and benedictions are not the only blessings. Ministry is blessing, and we can bless people at other times and in other forms. Words can be a form of blessing. We can enrich others with words of hope and comfort. There are people defeated or on the brink of defeat who need your blessing.

In fact, blessing can change the life of the one who blesses. I knew a young man who was bright but whose ministry was scarred by his criticism and sarcasm. When confronted about this, he acknowledged that he knew it was a problem and asked how he could overcome it. I suggested that he intentionally affirm three people everyday. Later he told me that affirming three people a day had been the most difficult discipline in his life but that it had changed his whole ministry and even his marriage.

I recall the first man who ever said to me, "Doran, I love you." That is not customary in our society. But what an affirmation; what a blessing. And ministry is . . . blessing.

Touch is a way to bless. I have seen people struggle to get where they could shake hands with the president or the pope as he passed by. The touch was a form of blessing. This is why the custom arose for ministers to greet people at the door as they leave a worship service. It also explains the laying on of hands at ordination. Touching is a way of blessing.

I had been pastor of a church but a few weeks when a deacon's son was fatally injured. As a young minister I wondered what to say to the family. Morris Ashcraft had served as interim pastor and had become close to the grief-stricken family. They knew that Ashcraft had lost a son a few years earlier. He was conducting a series of services in a nearby town, so I picked him up to go with me to visit the suffering parents. When we entered the home, Ashcraft put his arms around each parent for several minutes without saying a word— only three faces with tears. That moment I learned about the blessing of touch. And ministry is . . . blessing.

Blessing is also giving thanks. We have made interchangeable "saying a blessing" and "giving thanks" at meals. Apparently Luke preserved a pattern of Jesus. Luke 9:16 reports about Jesus: "And taking the five loaves and the two fish he looked up to heaven, and

blessed and broke them, and gave them to the disciples
to set before the crowd."

The story of the Last Supper shows Jesus offering a
blessing. Luke 22:17 tells that Jesus "took a cup, and
when he had given thanks he said, "Take this, and
divide it among yourselves.' " Two verses later "he took
bread, and when he had given thanks he broke it and
gave it to them, saying, 'This is my body which is given
for you. Do this in remembrance of me." Matthew's
account of this (26:26) makes the relationship between
thanks and blessing clear: "As they were eating, Jesus
took bread, and blessed, and broke it, and gave it to the
disciples and said, 'Take, eat; this is my body.' "

Parents know the blessing of having a grateful child
thank them for an act of kindness, duty, or gift. It
makes all the hardship, anxiety, and suffering worth it.
Ministers have been blessed by those to whom they
have ministered when those persons expressed thanks
to the ministers. All have the power to minister by
giving thanks. It is no wonder that one of Paul's most
repeated phrases was "thanks be to God." Ministry is
. . . blessing.

Blessings and Grace

Why don't we do better at giving blessings? I suspect
a major reason is our innate sense of wanting to trust
ourselves instead of grace. Works salvation is easy to
deny but difficult to quit practicing. We tend to see a
blessing as a reward for something someone does rather than being the gift of grace. Our typical logic is to
say, "What if I bless someone this week and they do
something wrong next week?" Grace is never deserved,
or it would not be grace. Blessing comes from grace, not

works. When we affirm and bless people we are the instruments of God's grace rather than his appointed judge to determine if they deserved the blessing.

We are ministers by our calling (God's grace) and ministry is . . . blessing.

6
Ministry Is . . . Redeeming

———————— ❤ ————————

Father Divine has been quoted as saying, "Metaphysicians have to learn how to tangibilitate." Like Father Divine I find things more easily understood when I make them tangible. It is helpful to me to take abstract concepts and put them in story form or present them as ordinary actions. Redeeming is a lofty concept. How can I make it tangible? I think of redeeming as taking something of little value and making it of great value.

Once my grandparents took an old rocking chair which had been stored for years in a neighbor's woodshed. The chair was broken and the many layers of varnish had eroded unevenly over the years. My grandparents took the chair, repaired the rounds, restrung the webbing, removed all the old varnish, and restained and revarnished it. They had restored a beautiful antique. They had taken something of little value (it was destined to be wood for a fireplace) and made it of great value—a fine antique rocking chair. They had redeemed the chair.

I have a friend in New Orleans who finds cars which have been junked and restores them. The cars are dented and rusted on the outside and torn up on the inside.

They won't run. He spends months and money restoring them until they are gleaming antiques worth thousands of dollars. He redeems the cars.

The word for redemption in the New Testament means "to buy." The computer I am using to type this manuscript was in boxes in a storeroom. I bought it and now I am using it. It was of no use in the boxes in the storeroom, but now I have made it a useful and valuable instrument. In a real sense I have redeemed it.

This is what God did. He paid the price in Jesus Christ on the cross to redeem us. He paid the price to take us, who were of little worth, and made us to have eternal worth.

The background of the word *redeem* in religion relates to the pagan notion of redeeming slaves. In the oracles of Delphi there is written the example of a woman who was a slave. She went to the priests of the pagan temple, paid the money for buying her freedom, and said that she had been bought by the god Apollo. Of course, in reality, she had paid the price herself; no god had given any thing toward the purchase price. The apostle Paul spoke of God purchasing us out of our slavery. He compared and contrasted human slavery and belonging to God.

"But if you can gain your freedom, avail yourself of the opportunity. For he who was called in the Lord as a slave is a freedman of the Lord. Likewise he who was free when called is a slave of Christ. You were bought with a price; do not become slaves of men" (1 Cor. 7:21-23, RSV).

Paul keeps the tension between slavery and freedom. We are free in God but belong to him. Another important difference between Christian and pagan redemption is that Christ paid the price for our redemption, while pagan gods offered no redemption price. In Romans Paul pointed out, "But God shows his love for us in that while we were yet sinners Christ died for us" (Rom. 5:8).

God's grace redeems us from the law. Paul wrote: "Christ redeemed us from the curse of the law" (Gal. 3:13, RSV). Later in Galatians he wrote, "But when the time had fully come, God sent forth his Son, born of woman, born under the law, to redeem those who were under the law, so that we might receive adoption as sons" (Gal. 4:4-5, RSV). A practice in the Roman world was for a man who had no son to purchase a promising slave and adopt the slave as a son. The slave became an adopted son and inherited the estate. This is probably Paul's reference since he went on to state, "So through God you are no longer a slave but a son, and if a son then an heir" (Gal. 4:7, RSV). Through God's grace we have been bought from the slavery of the law and are now made the sons of God. This was no "cheap grace," for the price for buying our freedom was the cross of Jesus Christ.

My father liked telling the old story of the boy and his boat. The boy and his father built a large model boat. The boy liked to take the boat out to the nearby lake and watch it sail on the water. One day a strong wind arose and carried the boat far out on the lake. The boy ran to the other side of the lake to retrieve the errant boat, but he could not find it. In panic he went to the house to get his father's help. They searched until dark but never found it. A few days later the boy was walking down the street and saw his boat in the window of a pawn shop. He returned home, got some money, and bought the boat. On the way home with the boat under his arm, he said, "I made you; now I bought you. You are really mine."

That is a parable of God's redeeming us. He made us. We were of value because we were made in the image of God; but because of our sin, we were of less value. Then God sent Jesus, His Son, as the price to be paid to redeem us from the slavery of the law and our sin. He made us and He bought us.

Paul applies the idea that redemption is taking something of some value and making it of greater value to "the redemption of our bodies" (Rom. 8:23, RSV). In 1 Corinthians 15 Paul went to great length to explain the resurrection as the changing from terrestrial to celestial bodies. He said: "So it is with the resurrection of the dead. What is sown is perishable, what is raised is imperishable. It is sown in dishonor, it is raised in glory. It is sown in weakness, it is raised in power. It is sown a physical body, it is raised a spiritual body" (1 Cor. 15:42-44, RSV).

The redemption of the body is the transforming of the physical body into a spiritual body. This is the process of taking an object of some value and making it into one of greater value.

The Ministry of Redeeming

The church has the ministry of redeeming. Christians are bearers of the grace of God and lead people to find their redemption bought by Jesus Christ. Rob Springs is a church-starting intern at Golden Gate Baptist Theological Seminary. He worked to start a new church in Point Richmond, California. One of the first

persons he led to Christ in the new mission was a teen-
age girl who said, "Like Jesus came to tell the world
about God, you've come to Point Richmond to tell us
about Jesus." In her own way she saw Rob Springs as
a minister of redemption.

We are ministers of redemption of the human as well
as the divine. Christian theology speaks not only of
salvation but also of sanctification. People need to be
redeemed from all that enslaves them. Don Dent had
served as a missionary to Malaysia and was returning
to the mission field to serve in Singapore. He told the
story of Suchi, a Malaysian Christian. After a church
service some nationals and several missionaries were
on the way home. The car suddenly went into a ditch.
They had tried for an hour to get the car out when Don
heard Suchi say, "Praise the Lord." When Don asked
the meaning of his praise, Suchi replied that two years
ago he wouldn't have been down in the ditch because
he wasn't a Christian and believed that there were evil
spirits in water and darkness. He said, "Now I'm not
afraid of darkness." Suchi had been redeemed from the
slavery of the fear of darkness.

People need to be redeemed from bad habits, evil
thoughts, and wrong motivations. People are in the
slavery of drink, lust, greed, and fear. Our ministry of
redemption is to help people out of their human slavery (which is also related to their spirituality). The
alcoholic has value because he or she was made in the
image of God, but he needs the greater value that
comes by redeeming him from slavery to drink.

Shortly after moving to a new pastorate, I met a lay
preacher who was a member of another denomination.

He was a respected accountant in the town. Later I learned that a member of the church where I was pastor had gone to a nearby city and found the man in the drunk tank. He bailed the man out, gave him a job, and helped him back to sobriety. This is the ministry of redemption. Ministry is . . . redeeming.

No one is worthless in God's sight. Jesus came to save sinners, not the worthless. Yet in all our lives there is so much that needs to be redeemed—we need to take those things that are of some value and make them worth so much more. The minister who counsels with a couple about their marriage is a minister of redemption. The minister who helps people make their marriages more worthwhile is redeeming. Ministry is . . . redeeming.

Ministers counsel youth about their careers, their character, and a college decision. This is done in the hope of the youth making their lives more worthwhile. Ministry is . . . redeeming.

I read where an American journalist spent time with the celebrated artist Picasso. Before leaving, the journalist expressed great admiration for Picasso's work although admitting that on his salary he could never afford one of Picasso's paintings. Picasso asked if the journalist had a dollar bill. The journalist gave Picasso a dollar bill. Picasso drew on it and said, "Now that dollar is worth much more because Picasso drew on it."

That is the way with our lives. They are not worthless because we were made in the image of God. But when God writes on our lives, they are worth so much more. That is redemption. A check is only a piece of paper worth very little until we write on it and sign.

Then the paper becomes worth so much more. Our ministry is to see that God's grace is written across the lives of people and that people live with the riches of that grace. Ministry is . . . redeeming.

7
Ministry Is . . . Reconciling

Ed Asner plays the part of a father estranged from his son (and somewhat from all the family) in a television play. One son had fled to Canada rather than serve in the Vietnam War. Now married and a father himself, he returns at Christmas not knowing how his father will receive him. Knowing that he has a fatal disease and a short time to live, the father reaches out to the family and lets them touch him during the Christmas season and effects family reconciliation.

The story is not empty sentimentalism but is symbolic. Christmas is the story of reconciliation. The angel announced that the Christ-child would be called "Emmanuel (which means, God with us)" (Matt. 1:23, RSV). Humanity and divinity were no longer separated but united in the person of Jesus Christ. Reconciliation took place in Bethlehem, was intensified at the cross, bore the first fruits in the resurrection, and awaits fulfillment in the Kingdom of God.

Nothing hurts worse than to be at odds rather than at peace with someone. I have officiated at weddings and funerals where icy stares drowned out all my words. Jesus knew this. Peter had denied the Lord three times. Peter experienced the terrible estrangement which guilt brings when the Lord looked at him as He was being taken to the judgment hall to face Pilate. I wonder if this is not the reason for the angel at the empty tomb telling the women to "go tell his disciples and Peter" that he was going to meet them in Galilee. Jesus was announcing reconciliation to Peter.

Jesus was always a reconciler. The Pharisees tried to put distance between themselves and sinners, but Jesus talked and ate with them. Lepers had to stay a safe distance away, but Jesus approached them and healed them. The Pharisees had disdain for the common man, but Jesus even recruited fishermen to be his disciples. Jewish leaders ostracized tax collectors, but Jesus ate with them and called one to be his disciple. Jesus sought fellowship where others sought enmity. Jesus' ministry was reconciliation.

God and Humanity Reconciled

A great reconciliation happened between God and humanity through Christ. The apostle Paul wrote some of his most eloquent words to the Roman Christians about this. He said: "For if while we were enemies we were reconciled to God by the death of his Son, much more, now that we are reconciled, shall we be saved by his life. Not only so, but we also rejoice in God through our Lord Jesus Christ, through whom we have now received our reconciliation" (Rom. 5:10-11, RSV).

Paul also addressed reconciliation clearly in the Ephesian epistle. "For he [Christ] is our peace, who has made us both one, and has broken down the dividing wall of hostility, . . . [that he] might reconcile us both to God in one body through the cross, thereby bringing the hostility to an end" (Eph. 2:14,16, RSV). Paul was pointing out that Christ's ministry is reconciliation.

The old English word for reconciliation was *atonement,* which came from the combination of the three words "at-one-ment." There are many theories of the atonement, but each points to the reality of the reconciling ministry of Jesus Christ. The need for at-one-ment (togetherness in modern idiom) was why Paul wrote, "But now in Christ Jesus you who once were far off have been brought near in the blood of Christ" (Eph. 2:13, RSV).

Reconciliation was no accident but the purpose of God in sending His Son into the world ("For God so loved the world that he gave his only begotten Son . . ."). Reconciliation on the divine or human level never "just happens." It is always purposeful with risks and a price to pay. Jesus risked the cross and paid the price of reconciliation.

Nowhere in Jesus' ministry did he state the at-one-ment more clearly than in his prayer for the disciples in John's Gospel: "I do not pray for these only, but also for those who believe in me through their word, that they may all be one; even as thou, Father, art in me, and I in thee" (John 17:20-21, RSV).

Jesus' intent was reconciliation, and it could only happen in him. When we are in Christ, we are one in Him as the Father was in Christ and Christ in the Father (John 17:21). The reconciliation of God and humanity happened in Jesus Christ. As Karl Barth put it when speaking of reconciliation, "Jesus, God for man" and "Jesus, man for God." Only in the divine-human Jesus could reconciliation take place and humanity be reconciled to God. Jesus' ministry was reconciling.

The Church's Ministry of Reconciliation

The church has the ministry of reconciliation as part of its calling by God. Paul wrote: "All this is from God, who through Christ reconciled us to himself and gave us the ministry of reconciliation; that is, in Christ God was reconciling the world to himself, not counting their trespasses against them, and entrusting to us the message of reconciliation. So we are ambassadors for Christ, God making his appeal through us. We beseech you on behalf of Christ, be reconciled to God" (2 Cor. 5:18-20, RSV).

The church has a great task, for the hostility toward God is still very apparent. People deny God and many more deny his ways. It seems at times that Michaelangelo's painting on the ceiling of the Sistine Chapel in the Vatican seems prophetic. God reaches out for humanity, but the hands don't quite touch. Separation continues. The role of the church is not to decry the separateness but to be ambassadors for God calling people to be reconciled to God. Ministry is . . . reconciling.

The enmity between humanity and God is reflected in the enmity among the members of the human race. There is enmity between nations, tribes, clans, political parties, and families. The church's ministry of reconciling humanity to God continues on to be a reconciling force among people. Jesus spoke of human reconciliation. In the Sermon on the Mount Jesus warned about the consequences of human enmity: "But I say to you that every one who is angry with his brother shall be liable to judgment" (Matt. 5:22, RSV).

A few verses later Jesus counsels for reconciliation: "So if you are offering your gift at the altar, and there remember that your brother has something against you, leave your gift there before the altar and go; first be reconciled to your brother, and then come and offer your gift" (Matt. 5:23-24, RSV).

Peace (*shalom*) was the ideal and hope of Israel. They greeted each other by saying *shalom*. They named their holy city with the word (*salem* of Jerusalem was a form of *shalom*). Paul pleaded with the Ephesian Christians to "maintain the unity of the spirit in the bond of peace" (Eph. 4:3, RSV). The church is to spread this peace through its ministry of reconciling. Paul even spoke of the reconciliation of husbands and wives (1 Cor. 7:11).

When a minister does marriage counseling, there is an element of reconciliation with the hope of creating the condition of peace (*shalom*) in the family. All the counseling techniques which have been created only serve to fulfill the goal of creating peace (*shalom*). The counseling style and the needs of the people may vary, but the role of the Christian minister is to be a reconciler. Ministry is . . . reconciling.

Churches often need reconciliation. Divisions within churches create distance in fellowships. A church had been a model small-town church until a new minister arrived and began to create chaos in the church by dividing the church into "super saints" and "super sinners." Probably neither group deserved the title. Three divisions developed in the church, and the breach became so serious that the pastor had to leave. The next pastor had none of the flair or gift of oratory of the previous pastor, but he had what the church needed— the ministry of reconciliation. After ten years of his ministry the church was again a fellowship. Reconciliation had taken place. Ministry is . . . reconciling.

I heard of an incident that took place in a church in a southern city. The church had been located downtown but moved to the suburbs when blacks began to populate their neighborhood. They faced another crisis because blacks were beginning to move into their new area. The question arose as to whether they should admit blacks into the church. The business session of the church had lasted for hours with many emotional speeches pro and con.

When they were about ready to vote, a man got up from the back of the church and walked toward the microphone. He was one of the beloved saints of the church and had not spoken. He had been a merchant near the old church site. He had been robbed and beaten three times by blacks and the last time left for dead. Although he was elderly, he survived; but he had to use a cane as he limped down the aisle of the church. Everyone wondered what he would say.

When he got to the microphone he began to sing, "Jesus loves the little children, all the children of the world. Red and yellow, black and white, they are precious in his sight. Jesus loves the little children of the world." He said no more. The church voted to admit "all the children of the world." Ministry is . . . reconciling.

Communities need the church's ministry of reconciliation. Communities experience class against class, race against race, and political party against political

party. Justice becomes impossible and progress
becomes mired in the mud of mindless controversy.
While the church has ideals to uphold, it also has the
ministry of reconciliation to fulfill.

J. Alfred Smith is pastor of the Allen Baptist Temple
in Oakland, California. During the social upheaval of
the 1960s his voice was the voice of reason which held
the community together. He was later recognized by
the city as one of its heroes. Ministry is . . . reconciling.

The word used in the New Testament for reconciliation literally means "change." Where there is change,
someone has to pay the price for the change. The cross
was the price for our eternal reconciliation. Wherever
there is human reconciliation, there is a price. The
price may be pride, egos, and hurts. The ministry of
reconciliation exacts a price. The price is not usually
dollars and cents but personal.

Three young men were trying to start a church in a
San Francisco community which had been Russian
speaking for generations. The church had remained
Russian speaking although most of the community
now were English speaking. The three young ministers
met with the council of the Russian church, hoping
that they would expand their ministry to the English-
speaking people in the community.

Toward the close of the meeting an elderly man,
Henry, spoke to the group in heavily accented syllables
but with words more eloquent than the young men had
probably ever heard. Henry had been born in Russia
before the revolution. His father had been a wealthy
merchant philanthropist. When the revolution came,
the authorities took their business and their house and
told them that they were enemies of the state. Henry's

words to the young men were: "Too many lonely people. Too many. They want part of your heart, part of
your soul."

That is the price that has to be paid to bring people
from loneliness to reconciliation; you have to give them
a part of your heart and soul.

William Barclay said, "The task of the preacher is to
break men's hearts at the sight of the broken heart of
God."[1] Ministry is . . . reconciling.

Note

1. William Barclay, *William Barclay: A Spiritual Autobiography*
(Grand Rapids: William B. Eerdmans Publishing Co., 1977), p. 106.

8
Ministry Is . . . Remembering

"Precious Memories" is the title of a song. The reason for its popularity is that it touches one of the powerful human capacities—remembering. All persons have special times which they remember. Some memories are joyful; others hurt but are nonetheless powerful. We have the joyful memories of the birth of a child and the painful memories when we lost loved ones in death. Every family has its photo album and scrapbook. Many keep journals of trips. These are ways we remember those special occasions in our lives.

The Greeks and Hebrews both emphasized the role of remembering. However, the Greeks remembered ideas while the Hebrews remembered history. Some scholars interpret the Old Testament as being Israel's recital of the special events between Israel and God.

The first speech of Moses after God's people escaped Egypt was, "Remember this day, in which you came out from Egypt, out of the house of bondage" (Ex. 13:3, RSV). This was a significant time and transition in Hebrew history, so it was remembered and ritualized. The ritual which grew out of the people's remembering the escape from Egypt was the Passover.

One day a week was a special day of remembrance of

God. One of the Ten Commandments was "Remember the sabbath day, to keep it holy" (Ex. 20:8). God created the world and God's people created a weekly ritualizing of their blessings from God.

The Hebrews remembered special people in their history. During a crisis in the wilderness, Moses exhorted the people to "Remember Abraham, Isaac, and Israel [Jacob]" (Ex. 32:13, RSV). The celebration of Purim was begun to remember Esther and her heroism during one of Israel's crises.

Remembering was important to the early Christian church. Jesus provided the ritual for remembering during the Last Supper. He gave the disciples bread, symbolizing his broken body, and said to them, "This is my body which is given for you. Do this in remembrance of me" (Luke 22:19, RSV). The church did remember. As far away as Corinth Paul taught the Christians, "This is my body which is for you. Do this in remembrance of me" (1 Cor. 11:24, RSV). The saving death of Christ is still remembered and ritualized in the Lord's Supper in the church.

Remembering is important. We have all heard that those who don't remember the mistakes of history are condemned to repeat them. The church is the repository of remembrances. This is one reason why the Old Testament is important; it is our record of our roots and our God in history. The Christian church remembers its past—its beginning in Jesus Christ and its development under the Holy Spirit.

The Bible is the special book of remembering. Some things are too important to be left to oral tradition. God inspired the Scriptures to be the special book of remembrances for the Christian church. The Christian church

also remembers its future because the resurrection of
Jesus belongs to the first fruits of our future resurrection.

Remembering is an important function of the Christian church. When the Christian church reaches out to
evangelize the world, it does not give the world a message about itself but shares with the world the remembrances of Jesus Christ. When the Christian church
addresses the problems of the world, it remembers and
relates the ethics of Jesus' message to the contemporary problems. Ministry is . . . remembering.

Remembering is important because of change and
transition. The Hebrews left Egypt and how quickly
they forgot! New generations were born and needed to
remember. They moved into Canaan and needed to
remember. The same was true of the Christian church.
New converts came into the church. The missionary
movement took Christianity outside of Palestine. The
apostles died. The church needed to remember.

The way the human race remembers is by developing
rituals. Every nation has its special holidays which are
ways to ritualize important events. Every nation has
its monuments and every religion its shrines as a way
of ritualizing remembering. Stained-glass windows in
medieval churches depicted the life of Christ so illiter-
ate people could learn and remember the life of Christ.
Some churches follow a "church year" to assure that
the important events in the life of Christ and the Christian church are remembered.

Changes and transitions are difficult, so remembering and rituals help. Children provide a good illustra-
tion. Making the transition from playtime to bedtime
is difficult for children. My wife and I used to "ritualize

the transition." We would sit on the couch with our daughters and read them a story. (When the grandparents came, they would join us and one of the girls would say, "Grandpa, 'member us a story.") After the story was a "horsey" ride around the dining room table with each girl taking her turn on my shoulders, which culminated in my dumping her on her bed. They had been through the bedtime ritual and were ready (usually) for bed.

Remembering helps transition. Jesus remembered Scripture in his last moments on the cross (Ps. 22:1). Stephen, while being stoned, looked into the heavens and saw "the glory of God, and Jesus standing at the right hand of God" (Acts 7:55, RSV). Paul and Silas sang when jailed.

The rituals we develop help us through the difficulties and hurting times of life. The ministry of the church is to ritualize the special transitions of people's lives so they may pass through them with significant memories. The Passover ritualized the Exodus. John the Baptist's baptism ritualized a new era among God's people—the coming of the Messiah. The Lord's Supper ritualized the saving event of the cross. Observing rituals is a way the church ministers by remembering.

While I don't subscribe to the Roman Catholic view of the sacraments, they have taken seriously remembering by ritualizing transitions. The first transition in life is birth, and Roman Catholics ritualize it with baptism. They have been able to do this because there is something deep within the human heart which wants to ritualize birth. This is the power behind celebrating birthdays. I have been in churches which would never consider baptizing an infant but each Sunday recognize those celebrating birthdays. The urge to ritualize the transition of birth has led to dedicating babies in churches which oppose infant baptism.

The transition from childhood to adolescence (the beginning of adulthood) is ritualized among Roman Catholics through the sacrament of confirmation. In evangelical churches this has been the time when youth traditionally make their confession of faith in Christ and are baptized.

Marriage is the sacrament which ritualizes the transition into adulthood and from singleness to mutuality. The rituals of the wedding differ from culture to culture, but they are universal. Ritualizing a transition fulfills the need of the heart.

Roman Catholics have also ritualized the final human transition, death, with what formerly was called extreme unction. The bereaved have a ritual of the funeral to mark the transition of a loved one from life to death. The funeral is universal although the form of the ritual differs according to culture. However, few traditions have developed ways of helping the dying person ritualize the transition. This has become especially difficult in the day of modern medicine where machines and medicine supplant the minister.

Confession, now called the rite of reconciliation, ritualizes the transition from an unholy state to a state of forgiveness. The theology implicit in this is rejected by many Christians who recognize the need to confess sins. A minister who uses Christian principles in counseling sees people passing through the transition of living with guilt to living with forgiveness.

What I have been trying to do is to show the need of the human heart for rituals when facing the transitions of life. It is the need of remembering which is a ministry of the church. People go through many other transitions which require attention. This is an era marked by many transitions. We live in a mobile society where few of us live in the town where we were born. Vocations are in transition. We are told that we need to retrain every fifteen years for a new vocation. Jobs that looked secure a generation ago no longer exist. The revolution in technology creates transitions faster than we can keep up with them. A new computer is marketed every week. The church has a monumental task helping people through the transitions of life.

A major transition in American society is moving. In tests developed to measure stress, one of the items with the highest points of stress is moving. It brings about all kinds of changes: friends, family, school, doctors, dentists, jobs, and church. Studies have shown that when people move they are less likely to become involved in church if they wait more than six weeks to do so. How can the church help to ritualize the transition of moving?

When Ernie White was pastor in St. Joseph, Missouri, he found that members who moved from St. Joseph often experienced difficulty getting involved in a new church. He developed a ritual whereby he invited the persons who were about to move to come to the front of the sanctuary at the close of a worship service. He recounted (remembered) their involvement in the church, their special experiences and service in the church. He gave them a missionary charge to become involved in God's work soon where they were going. He offered them the church's continuing concern and remembrances and offered a prayer for them. Dr.

White found this was an effective ritual to help people make the transition from one church to another.

School is a major transition in our society not only for students but also for parents. I remember my wife standing in the driveway crying as our first daughter marched up the street to catch the school bus on her first day of school. Graduation can be just as traumatic. The graduating student faces uncertainty and new roles, while the parents realize that they have come to an end of an era. There is a place for a significant ministry in the transitions of entering and graduating.

In our society engagements for marriage (and broken engagements) are significant transitions. There is stress because of new levels of relationships, decisions, and the beginning of molding lives together. This is a time for persons to remember who they are, their heritage, and their spiritual commitments. A ritual of transition can be meaningful.

Unfortunately, some marriages end in divorce. It is a time of hurting and needs. As the ritual of a wedding ceremony helps a person to formalize the reality of the new state of marriage and what is expected in marriage, a ritual for someone who has divorced helps to heal the hurts and to anticipate a positive response to life in the future. This ritual of transition helps persons to bring closure of their feelings and open a new vision for their worthwhileness in the future.

A health crisis is a time for the ministry of transition. A person suffering a health crisis may realize that life will never be completely the same again. Even when people regain their health, they have faced the reality of their frailty. One reason why a hospital min-

istry is so important for the pastor is because of the
need of people to reflect on (remember) their humanity.

A job crisis is also a time when people need the ministry of ritualizing transitions. Changes in technology,
the economy, and health create many job changes.
Wherever there is change, there is loss. Part of the loss
may be in persons' self-esteem. They need to remember. Retirement is a very significant transition. People
who have been productive and part of an organization
suddenly find the next day the world can do without
them. The result can be a spiritual crisis. They need
the ministry of ritualizing the transition.

Change Means Loss

An axiom says that change means loss. This is true
even when the change is for the better. Because change
means loss, periods of uncertainty are critical times for
people. The story of Lot's wife instructs us. Fleeing the
sinful city, she looked back and turned into a pillar of
salt. Remembering is necessary; looking back is deadly.
Anger arises out of transition. People ask why they
have to change to reach goals. This happens when
households move in order for a parent to take a new job
or technology requires an employee to change.

There is great stress in transition. Statistics show
that major illnesses often follow within months of a
move. An adage of my grandmother was that three
moves was as bad as a fire. Coping mechanisms we had
in one job or community may not work in a new one.

There is the loss of the sacred in transitions. We lose
special people. I remember coming home one night
finding my daughter in my study sobbing. She angrily
said, "Why do we have to move. I'm losing all my

friends and my school." We also lose special places
which have become important to us: school, house,
church. We often fail to realize until we are threatened
with a move that places have become shrines to us.
Transition also may mean the loss of special functions.
When an elderly person moves into a nursing home, he
or she may lose privacy or the ability to go next door
and see an old friend, use the telephone, or decide on
what the next meal will be.

The Ministry of Remembering

The ministry of remembering comes through the
ritualizing of transitions—whether these are special
seasons like Christmas and Easter, special services
such as baptism and the Lord's Supper, or related to
the contemporary human situation. The ministry intervention must be appropriate if it is effective. Sometimes a minister calls on a parishioner in the hospital
but seems to make a social visit rather than a pastoral
call. An appropriate ritualization of the transition
needs to have three things: recital, blessing, and a symbol.

Recital is remembering. Persons may need to remember past victories, health, blessings, or contribu-
tions to others. They may need to remember elements
of their Christian life and faith in Christ. They may
need to remember their heritage. The minister may
recite these or elicit them from the person. Remembering heals the soul. Ministry is . . . remembering.

The minister blesses. The blessing may be in the
form of a prayer or an affirmation and should be direct
rather than oblique, heartfelt by the minister.

The ritualizing of transition needs to be symbolized.

The symbol should be appropriate to the situation. Often a symbol can be created for a given situation so that it reflects what is going on in the life of the person. The symbol should be a gift which is given to the person. Many times it can be a simple but tangible gift. A pastor may give a rose to a couple when a new child is born. A pastor may hand a card with a prayer on it to a patient in the hospital. There can often be participation in the symbol giving. The gift of the symbol may be from the church. The symbol may be oral. The pastor may say to a parishioner in the hospital or the home, "Before I go, I would like to read a Scripture. What passage would be meaningful to you?"

The church's ministry is to offer to the world the great remembrances of the faith. God has provided special rituals of baptism and the Lord's Supper and the inspired Scriptures to do this. Human situations provide the church with special opportunities to minister by ritualizing human transitions. Ministry is . . . remembering.

9
Ministry Is . . . Revealing

♥

"I have lived with that man for five years and I still don't know him." This was a statement by a wife in a troubled marriage. It really does happen. Some people have difficulty revealing themselves to others. Probably everyone has difficulty revealing themselves to someone.

God is a revealing God. He makes Himself known. He spoke through the prophets, the law, and the Scriptures. He also speaks through nature and history. He has revealed Himself through Jesus and the Holy Spirit.

The ultimate revelation of God was in Jesus Christ. Hebrews 1:1-3, RSV, says: "In many and various ways God spoke of old to our fathers by the prophets; but in these last days he has spoken to us by a Son, whom he appointed the heir of all things, through whom also he created the world. He reflects the glory of God and bears the very stamp of his nature."

God's fullest revelation of Himself was in the incarnation of Jesus Christ. The incarnation was God's picture of Himself to the world. If you want to know what God is like, look at Jesus. We do not argue that Jesus was divine because He was Godlike; we know what Godlike is because Jesus revealed it.

God became flesh in Jesus Christ to reveal Himself to the world in a way that He had never done before. Jesus was God; the medium was the message! Jesus revealed more of God than God had ever revealed before. God's coming as a human being made a fuller revelation possible. God wanted to reveal Himself as a person. Had God only wanted to give us better ideas, He could have given us a book or golden plates; but His full revelation meant that He had to come in human likeness.

God wants to reveal Himself to us. He wants us to know Him. The word *know* is important. We may know facts which are like computer data. We may know persons that way. We know their name, height, weight, job, habits, likes, and dislikes. The woman quoted in the first paragraph of this chapter probably knew her husband by this definition. She knew there was more to knowing than that factual knowledge. There is intimate, personal knowledge which she did not have with her husband. The Bible does not only use the word *know* to refer to facts but to an intimate kind of personal knowledge. *Know* is classically used in the Bible to refer to intimate sexual relationships. "Now Adam knew Eve his wife, and she conceived and bore Cain" (Gen. 4:1, RSV).

God not only wanted us to have facts about Himself but also personal and intimate knowledge of Him. God did not so much reveal facts about Himself in Jesus Christ as He revealed Himself. Jesus did not go on a lecture circuit to discuss the theological notions about God; He revealed Him.

The Greek gods were aloof, not letting people know where they resided or what they were planning. They often visited earth, according to the myths, using pseudonyms. The God of Jesus Christ wanted people to know Him and revealed Himself in Jesus Christ.

The Church Has the Ministry of Revealing

The Great Commission tells us to baptize, teach, and make disciples. Each of these involves intimate, personal knowledge of God. The commission of the church is not to saturate people with facts or brainwash people with behavior modification but to reveal God. The response of faith to revelation means a personal revelation which is intimate, personal knowledge.

The church reveals God to the world not only because of the command of the Great Commission but also out of love and concern. The faith response to the revealing of God enriches people's lives and molds their destinies. Our love comes from Jesus' love for us: "Greater love hath no man than this, that a man lay down his life for his friends" (John 15:13). We have concern for our fellow human beings. We give money for missionary enterprises to people we have never seen and in countries where we will never be. Why do we do it? We are concerned about others and want to reveal God to them in the fullest way possible.

The church reveals the mystery of God in Jesus Christ. Gnosticism, the early church heresy, claimed secret knowledge. Gnostics believed that it was only revealed to a few, and they did not share it except with a few of the specially chosen who would be initiated into their semisecret society. The Christian church opposed the Gnostic intrusion into Christianity because

they believed in revealing the real mystery of God as
God revealed it in Jesus Christ.

The Revealing Person

Jesus was a revealing person; others try to remain
hidden. Jesus remained open to others; some remain
closed to others. Jesus wanted to reveal and was honest
to God, self, and others. Jesus did not only reveal ideas
but Himself. The revelation of Himself was a far more
important revelation than any of his ideas. Most of the
ideas of Jesus preserved in the New Testament have
parallels in some form elsewhere, but what was unique
about Jesus' revelation was that He lived it and revealed truth in Himself.

The revealing person must be intentional. Certainly
we let other people see something of us whether we
intend it or not, but effective revealing requires intentionality.

A revealing person is an open person. The revealing
person does not hide behind others, ideas, institutions,
or customs. Revealing persons are open to others rather than shutting them out. Words may reveal or keep
people at a distance. The revealing person lets others
"inside them" and allows others to know their feelings
and their plans.

The revealing person is humble. As Jesus humbled
Himself and took the form of a servant, people who
reveal have to be humble servants. Rather than trying
to be aloof and superior, revealing people share themselves with others and, in this way, become the servants of others. Revealing people try to be *with* others,
not *over* others.

Revealing is giving clues to the mystery of life. It is

offering the key to the riddle of life. I recall Professor Jasper Clark lecturing on the molecular structure of physical properties. He opened a door to a new world for me. The world had been all around me in molecules, atoms, electrons, and protons; but no one had ever helped me to see them before. Professor Clark gave me a revealing clue about the world that day in chemistry class.

Revealing is also self-disclosure. The deepest level of revealing is not ideas but "our story." Revealing at its fullest occurs when we tell what has happened to us. The testimony of a Christian tells what the facts mean to him. Revealing is not an impersonal relating of impersonal data but one's personal involvement with facts through experience. Real revelation is of the heart as well as the head. The scholar may reveal the facts of the head, but the minister must reveal the experiences of the heart also. Ministry is . . . revealing.

Effective revealing communicates what is appropriate. The person to whom we are trying to reveal ourselves and our experiences must have a readiness for what we have to reveal. The child is prepared for only so much revelation. The apostle Paul could even tell the Corinthian Christians that he had to feed them as babes rather than as men who could take meat. There has been a fad of being "honest" with people which meant "telling all." I question whether this is honesty on the part of the confessor or the confessor's need for the dramatic or self-flagellation. Revealing meets the needs of the persons to whom we are revealing, not our own needs. My "telling" is not necessarily revealing. Revealing comes out of love and concern for others rather than fulfilling my own needs to startle or impress someone else. Revealing is to minister to the needs of others. Ministry is . . . revealing.

When Jesus Christ revealed God, He did not give statistics but revealed Himself. Self-revelation is essential in revealing. Self-revelation means that we must have some knowledge of who we are and be willing for others to peek behind the curtains of our lives and see us the way we really are, with all our glory and all our warts. Like Jesus, if we are going to reveal God to someone, we must also reveal ourselves since we are the bearers of the grace of God. The medium is the message for us too. God's grace is never abstract; it is incarnated. Revealing does not take place by coercion or upon the command of the receiver; revealing comes by grace. Since grace is a gift and is never abstract, Christians, as bearers of God's grace, reveal God by giving themselves to others.

Why would a person not want to reveal if he has experienced the grace of God? It is the fear of self-revelation. As one author put it, "Why am I afraid to tell you who I am?" There is the fear of intimacy. Some people have been taught to keep things to themselves and not to get close to others, while others have suffered hurts inflicted by others. When people reveal themselves they develop intimacy.

We may not reveal because of other risks involved in revealing. We may fear rejection. We may fear not saying things right. We may fear being misunderstood. These are the risks of revealing.

Failure to reveal may be our flight from responsibility. Once I reveal, I bear some responsibility for the revelation and what happens because of it. When I recommend a person to be the pastor of the church, I feel the responsibility for what I have done. We may feel the responsibility for revealing too heavily. We may ask, "What if I try to reveal and do so poorly that I turn others away?" Of course, everyone won't respond to our revealing with a faith response; but we risk revealing because of their need and our love and concern. Ministry is . . . revealing.

Revealing Also Distorts and Hides

Revealing distorts and hides as it reveals. The Book of the Bible called Revelation is a good example. The inspired writer wanted to reveal God's plan for people under persecution without the persecutors being able to understand it. (Unfortunately, Christians have had difficulty understanding it too.) Even with the fullness of the revelation of God in Jesus Christ, the Lord once said to his disciples, "I have yet many things to say to you, but you cannot bear them now" (John 16:12, RSV).

Revealing also distorts. The incarnation was the best medium of the revelation of God, but the doctrine of the trinity was necessary to emphasize that all of God was not revealed in Jesus Christ. The human is the bearer of only part of the divine. The most beautiful painting by an artist distorts reality for the purpose of communicating beauty. If you wanted a picture of a house, a photograph would be a more faithful representation of the physical structure. The artist distorts the reality in order to show a meaning which transcends the actual physical structure. However, even photographs distort. Whatever lens is on the camera distorts the light rays in a certain way. This is perhaps most obvious with the use of wide-angle lenses.

Language distorts. Language is finite and therefore

distorts the infinite when we try to reveal the infinite in finite language. We may use many eloquent words, but none can describe a mother's love for her child. Words are impersonal and inadequate bearers of the personal. We use words because they are often all we have to try to convey a message—a revelation. As one theologian put it, "We speak of God only not to be silent." Of course, we can't describe all of the eternal with temporal words, just as the finite cannot comprehend fully the infinite.

We have developed a kind of religious language in order to reveal God in metaphorical terms. These terms are special distortions. Those who are not acquainted with the distortions (religious language) will have difficulty with our attempts to reveal God to them. Their response is like the little boy who told his Sunday School teacher that he knew that God was left handed. When the Sunday School teacher asked how he knew, the little boy replied, "Because Jesus is sitting on his right hand."

Think of the difficulty a person might have listening to the description of a baseball game while taking the language literally. When the announcer says that someone stole second base, the listener could imagine a man with a gun held on the players while he escaped with the base from the playing field. When a player hits a home run, he usually doesn't run. When a player gets a walk, he usually doesn't walk. This special language makes sense to some but reveals distortions to others.

When we reveal, we distort because we tell our story. It is a personal story bounded by our personal gifts and history. Our revelations are distorted by cultural forms and history. The Old Testament commands us not to boil our kids (goats) in milk. That doesn't reveal much to most people. In past times and cultures that was a pagan religious practice.

The ministry of revealing is revealing God by self-revealing. But how can it be effective if it is distorted by the personal, the culture, history, language, and the person to who we are revealing? It is effective because the revealing is by grace.

10
Ministry Is . . . Investing

───────────────── ❤ ─────────────────

A friend and I often travel to meetings together. After checking in at the hotel, we stop by the paper vendors. I buy the latest edition of the local paper and my friend buys a copy of *The Wall Street Journal.* He buys *The Wall Street Journal* because he has investments in the stock market (I don't). He is looking about his investments.

Our investments are important to us. Jesus' parable about the owner of the vineyard sending servants and finally his son to collect what was due him carries the theme of investment (Luke 20:9-18). Jesus knew the meaning of the parable intimately since God is the Creator and Owner of the world in which He has invested and has sent His Son, Jesus, to care for the investment. The incarnation was God's investment in the world. He sent Jesus into the world to save the world. The world's rejection of Jesus was a rejection of God's investment.

The apostle Paul recognized investments. He went to Corinth and made his way making tents. Later he wrote to the Corinthian Christians asking them to open their hearts to him because he had taken advantage of no one. No wonder Paul's correspondence to the Corinthians is the longest of his we have in Scripture.

Christians Make Investments in Others

A minister I know had changed pastorates every two or three years. Shortly after arriving at one of these waystations in his mobile career, he told me: "I've moved around too much. I'm going to put my roots down and invest my life here." He told me that again about two years later in his next pastorate. An important ingredient in effective ministry is investing in the people where you are a minister. Of course, time is not the real issue; some can stay for several years and not invest in the lives of people.

Having served a good many churches as interim pastor, I believe the most serious credibility problem of ministers and the cause of cynicism among laypeople toward ministers is that they find ministers self-seeking rather seeking to invest in others. Once I pointed out to a deacon the low salary they had given their previous pastor, but the deacon replied: "If that is the way ministers treat people, they get too much now."

The issue is how much the minister identifies with the people and invests in them—time, energy, emotions, compassion, understanding, and suffering. Someone has said that you can tell a good shepherd; he smells like the sheep. That is identifying with and investing in the sheep! Ministry is . . . investing.

The minister needs to invest in what the people invest in. I was asked to speak to a Homecoming at a church. The pastor was very upbeat, bragging on the food, the fellowship, the music, the committee in charge of the Homecoming, and those who had worked

hard making preparations. He was obviously enthusiastic. Later he thanked me for coming and explained that he had not been happy about the
Homecoming when he became pastor. His first year at
the church he had even hinted that they shouldn't
have Homecoming but had met strong sentiment for
the tradition. He said that after the first Homecoming
he realized how much it meant to the people, so he tried
to make it the best event he could. This pastor had
learned about investments and invested himself with
his people.

As ministers we invest in the people's investments.
Their investments may be in a life-style. A blue-collar
church called a man as pastor who had been serving a
white-collar church in a plush suburb of New York
City. The new pastor carried with him the sophistica-
tion of his own life-style which had been enriched by
his previous pastorate. The congregation couldn't understand his sermons; they weren't simple, straightfor-
ward presentations of the gospel but classic pieces of
eloquence. The previous pastor had gone fishing with
deacons, but the new pastor preferred to go to meetings
of psychological associations and philharmonic con-
certs. While the new pastor was gifted, he never invested in the life-style of his congregation.

Ministers need to invest in the institutions in which
the congregation invests. The pastor who tried to do
away with the woman's missionary organization never
knew what happened to him. He had another plan of
missionary education and work, but it was only his.
The church was proud of their investment in the woman's missionary organization.

A pastor moved into the parsonage which was inadequate: plumbing, heating, and insulation problems aggravated him. He immediately campaigned to sell the parsonage and build a new one. He didn't understand the investments people had in that house. A few years before they had no parsonage. By sacrificial giving they bought the house. People of the church worked hard to make it livable. They knew its inadequacies but also knew their investments. The parsonage was a major reason the pastor didn't stay long.

The next pastor, wife, and several children moved into the parsonage and showed appreciation for it. They worked to decorate it and improve it. They kept the yard and planted flowers. He stayed longer than any other full-time pastor. He had invested in what the church had invested in.

People invest in ministries. The investment may be financial. I know of one Baptist association which wanted to divide and become two and another situation where two associations talked about merging. Neither was able to do so because of associational camps. People had invested in the camps and were afraid of losing their investment.

Where I was an interim pastor, a former church member returned to visit. He was reminiscing with one of the members about when his family attended the church. The member said to the visitor, "You invested a lot here." The former member replied, "I didn't have much money to invest, but I sure gave a lot of time." Time is also an investment that people make to ministry.

People also make emotional investments. I was pastor of a church which had contributed to a fund to build a new sanctuary for years. Finally we were about to begin. One night the church members met at the church to take out the pews, stained-glass windows, and other furniture. I walked into the old sanctuary and found an elderly lady standing in the doorway crying. I asked her what was wrong. She told me that she had been married in that old sanctuary, her dad's funeral had been there, and her two children had been baptized in the baptistry. She had made an emotional investment which I had not.

We Want Investments to Pay

When a person makes an investment in a business, he wants the investment to pay dividends. Christians who invest money, time, and emotions in ministries want their investments to pay off. When people invest in something, a sense of fellowship develops among those who have a common investment. They join together to nurse and protect their investment. Motivation comes from investing. If an idea is yours, few get excited about it. If others invest in an idea, they will get excited about it. When people develop an idea they have already invested in it.

When people invest, they will work and invest more to see that the investment pays dividends. When a congregation invests in a pastor, they want to see the pastor succeed. They want to know what and how the pastor is doing because they have an investment. They want to see results because they have invested.

The wise minister will take care of people's investments. The wise minister will not make light of the investments but protect them and try to enrich them. The minister may wish to invest another way, but that will have to wait until people see the minister take care

of their investments. The wise minister will invest in
the investments of others so they will have mutual
investments. It isn't always convenient to go to a Sunday School class picnic or to attend Rotary with a deacon, but the investments are important to others. A
good minister takes care of other's investments. Ministry is . . . investing.

When investments go sour, there will be problems.
People will need a scapegoat, and often that is the
minister. If the minister tries to make someone else the
scapegoat, people will fear and distrust the minister.

When there is a problem with investments, people
feel betrayed. The result is anger and grief. Many people had deep emotional investments in Martin Luther
King, Jr., and his movement. When he was assassinat-
ed, many felt betrayed and angry riots started around
the country.

Churches invest in their ministers. When a minister
fails to live a Christian life or fails to serve the church,
people feel betrayed. Good ministers invest in the people's investments and take care of people's investments. Ministry is . . . investing.

11
Ministry Is . . . Hoping

Dante wrote that the inscription over the gate entering Hell reads: "Leave every hope, ye who enter." Simply stated, hell is where there is no hope. There are people living on earth in a hopeless prison of existence. They are in hospitals, famine-stricken Africa, gulags of the world, and asylums. Some reach out a hand desperately trying to find what is the invisible thread of hope, having lost a home, mate, business, dignity, or wealth. The world often seems like the coal miners trapped by a cave in tapping out in Morse code, "Is there any hope?"

One day in our class, Wayne Oates told us: "Whatever you do as ministers, you must give hope." We must not throw the drowning anchors of despair but life jackets of hope. A painting was a mass of somber, dark colors swirling menacingly with one bright, glowing object in the middle—a cross! Ministers offer a ray of hope to the world threatened by personal, economic, social, and natural disasters. Ministry is . . . hoping.

The beautiful passage in 1 Corinthians 13 ends with the Christian trilogy "faith, hope, and love." Christian life cannot exist without hope. The church lives under the sign of the hope of Christ's resurrection. God is a hoping God. This is why He gave the law and sent the prophets and His Son. The Bible is a book of hope. Even in its darkest prophecy, the prophets spoke of a remnant from which would come the Messiah, the hope of the world. The Bible ends with a mysterious book whose message is that there is hope.

In classes and seminars I have asked each person to pick out a theological theme to use in theological reflection. Participants pick a variety of theological subjects each time, but I have noticed that in every group someone has chosen the subject of hope. No other theological theme has been chosen that consistently. I believe that is not accidental. We all struggle with the need for hope—in this world and the next.

Three years ago I prepared a sermon based on Barnabas on the subject of encouragement. Since it struck such a responsive chord in the first church where I preached it, I preached the sermon to other congregations. The typical response was for people to tell me how much they needed encouragement. There are so many people beaten down in life who need a minister to speak a word of hope. Ministry is . . . hoping.

The Power of Hope

How quickly good news spreads. Marletta, our daughter, recently left our home to return to Kansas City. As soon as she got a job, she called to tell us the good news. We want to tell good news. The word *gospel* is an old Anglo-Saxon word meaning good news. The gospel of Jesus Christ is the good news of God for the world. Christianity spread across the Roman Empire in one generation because the gospel of Christ was good news; it was hope. Pharisaism could never have done that because it was law and judgment. There is power in hope. Ministry is . . . hoping.

A minister-friend of mine was asked by a physician to make a special visit to one of his patients who was a parishioner of my friend. The physician said that there was no medical reason for her not to get well but that she was dying. My friend found that the patient thought that because of an event in her life, God would take her life. He pointed out the error in her logic and the graciousness of God, and she found hope. She lived. There is power in hope.

I have a book called *Great Lives, Great Deeds*. It is a book of brief biographies of scientists, statesmen, explorers, clergy, patriots, and artists. Looking for a common theme in their lives, I find only one: Each gave people a sense of hope. There is power in hope.

Hope is important for this world and the next. When a person is cornered without hope of escaping, he becomes more dangerous. Disenfranchised people feel cornered without hope. The reason for the creation of many Negro spirituals was the black sense of hopelessness in this world. They "looked over Jordan" for their only hope. Since the Lord is a God of justice, there is hope in this world. He is also Lord of the future, and there is hope in a world to come.

Recently I bought a plaque containing a saying reported to have been found in the basement of a Jewish ghetto after World War II. It says, "I know there is a sun even when it isn't shining. I know there is a God even when he is silent." The human race needs this inner sense of hope. It is natural to hope; yet lives are beaten down by the cruelties of life, and the flame of hope becomes hardly an ember. Christians have the gospel—the good news. Ministry is . . . hoping.

The Futility of False Hope

Liberal social thinkers and theologians at the beginning of the twentieth century believed that the human race had evolved to the point that there would never be another major war. World War I dispelled that false hope. Karl Barth told how he listened to the German guns from his church in Safenwill, Switzerland, and knew that his former liberal theology was wrong. It had offered false hope. There were those who believed that the Great War (World War I) was the war to end all wars. World War II dispelled that false hope.

The Old Testament knew about false prophets who offered false hopes. Elijah challenged them. Jeremiah mourned his people as they followed them. Amos railed against them. Paul warned against them. But they still appear offering their simplistic solutions to complex problems mounted in the frame of false hope.

Medical quacks with various kinds of snake oil still offer false hope to the desperately ill. The terminally ill, rather than making peace with human destiny, look for a ray of hope in medical quackery.

Recently I've been reading about some of the demagogues who appeared in the United States during the dark days of the Great Depression. Millions followed and supported them because they offered false hope. I was interested in the techniques of these demagogues. They spoke in generalities, pointed out "enemies" who were taking over the country, complained that people had been robbed of the privilege of setting their own destiny, and made radical promises if people would follow them. The demagogues knew the power of hope, but their promises were exercises in the futility of false hope.

There are pious preachers peddling false hope. James Jones founded Jonestown on false hope, and too many followed him. So many of these sound like the demagogues of the depression: identifying enemies, waving slogans of generalities, and offering promises to those who follow them—and doing it in the name of God.

The Helplessness of Hopelessness

In the movie "Oh God," God (disguised as George Burns!) says that his children need a little hope to help them get along in the world. That was one pearl of wisdom in the movie. There is helplessness in hopelessness. Ask the social worker and the physician about hopeless people and they will tell you that the hopeless feel helpless. Martin Marty in a recent book describes Christian living as a "wintry faith," but he does not feel helpless. The reason is in the brief sentence that ends the book: "One hopes."

Hopelessness is living by fate, not faith. People who believed in the Greek notion of the fate of the gods felt helpless. Paul believed in faith, not fate, and he had hope. While in prison he wrote: "Not that I complain of want; for I have learned, in whatever state I am, to be content. I know how to be abased, and I know how to abound; in any and all circumstances I have learned the secret of facing plenty and hunger, abundance and want. I can do all things in him who strengthens me" (Phil. 4:11-13, RSV). The man who wrote those words was a man of hope through faith, not a man helpless to fate.

Cynicism is born from hopelessness. The cynic does not believe the world can be changed and derides those who speak of hope. Doubt is not the great enemy of faith; but cynicism is. The real cynic distorts hope into illusion.

Injustice creates the helplessness of hopelessness. Persons suffering injustice feel as if they are playing cards with a stacked and marked deck.

The hopeless hate. They cannot trust in people or the future. Rage is their attempt to escape the helplessness of their hopelessness.

Viktor Frankl observed that people survived in concentration camps as long as they had hope. When they lost their hope, they soon perished.

Grace and Guilt

Hope comes by grace. Guilt is a state of hopelessness. Grace offers the hope of forgiveness. Guilt only offers condemnation and judgment. The good news (gospel) is an announcement of grace. The church goes into the world with the commandment to preach the gospel, the message of God's grace. It is a message of hope. Ministry is . . . hoping.

J. P. Allen once suggested that someone should write on "hope for the frogs." The hope for the frogs is that someone will kiss a frog and turn it into a prince. The Christian minister is in the business of "kissing frogs" so that the grace of God may turn them into princes. Ministry is . . . hoping.

Notes

1. *Great Lives, Great Deeds* (Pleasantville, New York: The Reader's Digest Association, 1964).

2. Martin Marty, *A Cry of Absence* (San Francisco: Harper & Row, Publishers, 1983).

12
Ministry Is . . . Showing Grace

The prologue of John's Gospel tells us, "And from his [Jesus'] fulness have we all received, grace upon grace. For the law was given through Moses; grace and truth came through Jesus Christ" (John 1:16-17, RSV). Jesus' ministry to the world was grace. The scribes and Pharisees were ready, as the law said, to stone a woman found in adultery. Jesus saved her but not by law. Only grace!

Guards came to Gethsemane to take Jesus. Simon Peter drew a sword to defend Jesus. Jesus told him to put it away because, if he wanted, his Father would send more than twelve legion of angels to protect him. Jesus would have been saved and the world would have been lost. Why didn't Jesus call for the legions? Only grace!

Simon Peter denied the Lord three times. Why did Jesus forgive him? Grace!

The Ministry of Law

God's ministers in the Old Testament mostly exercised a ministry of law. In fact, the word *grace* appears less than a dozen times in the Old Testament. The Jewish faith was faith in law and the God of law.

The issue of the place of law was one of the first crises faced by the Christian church. Early Christians took for granted that circumcision was necessary to be a Christian. Paul bitterly opposed it. He believed that circumcision and other works of law did not count toward salvation; it came by grace.

The ministry of law is a ministry of judgment. People who did not keep the law deserved judgment. There were rituals they could perform and if they did these works faithfully, they could escape judgment. There were people in the early church who continued in the law, making Christianity only a Jewish sect. This was a temptation at a time when Jews were exempt from persecution but not non-Jewish religions.

The Book of Hebrews seems to be a warning to Christians not to take this false and easy way out. Paul was certain that salvation from judgment was not by human works. When faced with the threat of those he called Judaizers, he said: "For by grace you have been saved through faith; and this is not your own doing, it is the gift of God—not because of works" (Eph. 2:8-9, RSV). The Christianity of Paul was based on the gift of God, not the works of humans. Christianity was grace, not judgment.

No generation of Christians has escaped an emphasis by some upon judgment. Some ministers still basically offer a ministry of judgment. We hear sermons which sound like judgment and condemnation with a paragraph of grace attached to the end. Justice is more nearly served by law than lawlessness, but in the end real justice comes from grace.

The Ministry of Grace

Christian ministry is the ministry of grace. In the final analysis it is not what humans make of themselves but the gift of God to us. The story of the Tower of Babel tells of humanity trying to reach God. Why was God displeased? Because God wanted to give humanity what they were taking in their own hands to do. God offered grace; the tower was the sign of works. Paul contrasted grace and works by saying we are "chosen by grace. But if it is by grace, it is no longer on the basis of works; otherwise grace would no longer be grace" (Rom. 11:5-6, RSV).

I have said at times that I believe in works instead of grace. Of course, I hold to a confession of faith that says that salvation is by grace rather than works. However, deep down inside of us, we want to be in charge of our own destiny rather than depend upon a gift. We work zealously to impress God with how worthy we are. Our ministry is likely to be frantic so we can get everything done that is necessary! Of course salvation is by grace; my head knows this, but how hard it is to get my heart to live by grace.

Salvation is by grace. Paul said it plainly: "For by grace you have been saved" (Eph. 2:9, RSV). Salvation is a gift. When we try to be good or go through certain rituals, we turn the gift into what we have earned and build the Tower of Babel all over again. Some have turned faith and repentance into works done to obtain salvation rather than their being grateful responses to the gift. When we try to get others to acknowledge the salvation by Christ, we offer them a gift rather than a way to earn their salvation.

The message of salvation is not telling about a secret road one can take to avoid judgment; it is an unconditional pardon by the governor of the universe—a gift. The difference between the message of *law* and *grace* is forgiveness. Law can only promise judgment; grace offers forgiveness. Grace offers hope, law, judgment. Ministry is . . . grace.

We are called by God's grace. Paul said that we are all called to belong to Jesus Christ by grace (Rom. 1:6; Gal. 1:6). Imagine our getting a phone call offering us a job for which we had not applied. God called us to discipleship. Paul also connected his call to apostleship with grace (Rom. 1:1-6) and believed that God "called me through his grace, was pleased to reveal his Son to me, in order that I might preach him among the Gentiles" (Gal. 1:15-16, RSV). Grace is the basis of our call to be a Christian and to be a minister. Ministry is . . . grace.

Grace enriches and strengthens us. We have various gifts from God which are examples of God's grace (Rom. 12:6). When we are weak and weary, God strengthens us by his grace. Paul paraphrases Isaiah 40:29 in saying, "My grace is sufficient for you" (2 Cor. 12:9, RSV). The Book of Hebrews urges us to go to the throne of grace and "find grace to help in the time of need" (4:16, RSV). We are often called upon to minister to those who have special needs and hurts. Ministry is . . . grace.

Healthy Ministry Is a Ministry of Grace

Don Gardner did a Doctor of Ministry project at a state mental clinic. He examined many people with mental and emotional problems who entered the clinic.

He checked on which ones had to return later and the kind of religion they had. He divided the people into three religious categories: healthy religion, unhealthy religion, and no religion. He defined healthy religion as characterized by love and forgiveness. He defined unhealthy religion as religion emphasizing law and judgment.

He found in his study that people with healthy religion were less likely to need to return to the clinic. People with unhealthy religion returned more frequently than those with healthy religion or no religion! Healthy ministry is the ministry of grace.

Grace should mean that we are gracious. Grace has no room for snobbery: social, education, or religious. Grace puts bitterness, vindictiveness, and cantankerousness to flight. Graciousness is an outward sign of inward grace. Ministry is . . . grace.

13
Ministry Is . . . Loving

─────────────── ♥ ───────────────

Love was the reason for Jesus' ministry—"For God
so loved the world. . . ." Jesus said that there was no
greater love than laying down one's life for a friend
(John 15:13) and proceeded on to the cross. Jesus' love
was evident in his ministry. He loved the disciples. He
loved Lazarus. He responded lovingly to Mary and
Martha, the ill, the bereaved, the sinners, and the disenfranchised.

Jesus Urged a Ministry of Love

Jesus' commandment was "that you love one another as I have loved you" (John 15:12, RSV). Jesus was in
one of His most intense moments of ministry to the
disciples when He gave them this commandment. The
early chapters of the Book of Acts show that they heard
His command and made their ministry loving one another. Paul urged his readers to love one another.

When a lawyer sought to test Jesus by asking what
he should do to inherit eternal life, Jesus asked him
how he read the law. The lawyer's answer was a quote
of Deuteronomy 6:5 about loving God and the addition
of Jesus to love "your neighbor as yourself" (Luke 10:
27, RSV; see also Mark 12:31). When the lawyer asked

who his neighbor was, Jesus translated the commandment into ministry and gave the parable of the Good Samaritan. The answer to Jesus' question about who showed mercy on the robber's victim was obvious. Ministry is . . . loving.

Jesus put the ministry of loving in radical terms. In the Sermon on the Mount, Jesus said: "You have heard that it was said, 'You shall love your neighbor and hate your enemy.' But I say to you, Love your enemies" (Matt. 5:43-44, RSV). Christian ministry reaches beyond our circle of friends and supporters to those separated from us by sin, life-style, theology, and ideology. We are to love our enemies. Ministry is . . . loving.

Jesus' Kind of Love

When we use the word *love* in the English language, we mean many different things. I may say that I love ice cream and my children, but I don't mean the same thing by those two usages. There are different kinds or levels of love.

The Greek language had four prominent words for love. One word was *eros,* from which the English word erotic is derived. Eros love meant to feel passionately about a person close to you whom you literally held in your arms. The Greek word *storge* was love for family and country. This is love for those who surround you and have some closeness to you. The word *philos* was brotherly love, which denoted a special, close friendship and relationship.

The word for God's love, and the love we are commanded to have, is *agape*. This kind of love is not only for those who are close to us but also love for those who are separated from us. Agape is God's kind of love. He is able to love us across the distance of the divine and human. He is able to love across the chasm of our sinfulness. Jesus' ministry demonstrated this. Paul emphasized it: "But God shows his love for us in that while we were yet sinners Christ died for us" (Rom. 5:8, RSV). Even when we were enemies, Christ died to reconcile us to God. Ministry is . . . loving with God's kind of love.

Caring As a Quality of Loving

"I love him, but I don't care what happens to him." The person who said that doesn't understand either loving or caring. God's kind of love is caring. This is why translators often use the word *loving-kindness* to translate one of the Hebrew words for love.

Caring is burden-bearing love. As we love others, we help them carry their load as Jesus did when He went to the cross to take on our burden of sin. We are to love others as ourselves. We take on their burdens as our own. Their burdens become our burdens. We treat their burdens as we treat our own. This also means that we must care for ourselves if we hope to care for others.

Caring requires risking. I have supervised Christian social-ministry interns who have worked distributing food to needy people. Interns always face the problem of whether people really are needy or are trying to con them. Often the interns are nearly paralyzed at first. They have to learn that caring requires risks. A man may care for a woman and get rejected. A woman may marry a man who divorces her. A couple may care for a child who rebels against them. When a person shows love by caring, he risks.

Love brings order and certainty into life. When you know someone cares, you know that he or she will look after you with love rather than betray you. A friend said recently, "I find fewer people I can trust anymore." He is in a position of power and influence. He has found that people want to manipulate him for what he can do for them rather than care for him and his work. Now he lacks a sense of certainty about people. My wife may confront me about things, but I never worry about her betraying me; she loves and cares for me. That gives me certainty and a sense of order in my life. It even enables me to risk, to love and care for others.

When a person is self-seeking rather than caring, he causes others to be closed and guarded. Two friends were listening to an eloquent man speak in a self-seeking manner. One friend whispered, "I don't trust him." Loving and caring opens others to us.

Wayne Wakefield was a deacon in a church where I was a pastor. He was a tough-minded man who stood firmly for his convictions about right and wrong. He had been a farmer until he retired, and his body was still muscular and strong from the heavy work. His fingers were twisted from an accident with a corn picker. Myrtle Wakefield was a dedicated Christian, a faithful wife, and as frail and delicate as Wayne was strong. One day I drove into their driveway and saw them under the shade tree. Wayne's twisted fingers and strong hands were braiding Myrtle's long hair with all the care a person could give. Loving is caring.

I may not have many gifts, but I can care. I may have

an excuse for not singing a solo, preaching a sermon, or administrating a program; but there is nothing to excuse me from not caring. Ministry is . . . loving.

And the Greatest of These . . .

Paul wrote the immortal love chapter of 1 Corinthians 13 about the priority of the ministry of love: "If I speak in the tongues of men and of angels, but have not love, I am a noisy gong or a clanging cymbal. And if I have prophetic powers, and understand all mysteries and all knowledge, and if I have all faith, so as to remove mountains, but have not love, I am nothing. If I give away all I have, and if I deliver my body to be burned, but have not love, I gain nothing" (1 Cor. 13:1-3, RSV).

Regardless of our many talents, they will not enhance our ministries without the ministry of love. However much we lack, the ministry of love will be effective.

Ministry is . . . love.